D0874709

Small Firms, *Big* Opportunity

How to Get Hired (and Succeed) in the New Legal Economy

LINDA CALVERT HANSON
SAMANTHA WILLIAMS

DB DecisionBooks
SEATTLE, WASHINGTON

Published by LawyerAvenue Press and its imprint, DecisionBooks

Cover design by Elizabeth Watson
Interior design by Rose Michelle Taverniti

Volume discounts available from LawyerAvenue Press. Email to editor@
LawyerAvenue.com.

Library of Congress Cataloging-in-Publication Data

Hanson, Linda Calvert.
 Small firms, big opportunity : how to get hired (and succeed) in the new
legal economy / Linda Calvert Hanson, Samantha C. Williams.
      p. cm. -- (The new lawyer survival guide ; v. 2)
 ISBN 978-0-940675-70-4 (alk. paper)
 1. Law--Vocational guidance--United States. 2. Lawyers--Employment--
United States. 3. Law firms--United States. I. Williams, Samantha C. II. Title.
 KF297.H325 2012
 340.023'73--dc23
                                        2012014324

CONTENTS

ABOUT THE AUTHORS

Linda Calvert Hanson is the Director of The Florida Bar's Henry Latimer Center for Professionalism, and the Chair of the General Practice, Solo and Small Firm Section of The Florida Bar. She formerly served as the Assistant Dean for Bar Success and Professionalism for over a year; as the Assistant Dean for Career Development for seven years both at the University of Florida College of Law and as the Assistant Dean for Professional Development at Florida Coastal School of Law. A graduate of University of Florida College of Law, Ms. Hanson has also practiced government and small firm law.

Samantha Williams is the Director of Employer Relations at the Sandra Day O'Connor College of Law at Arizona State University, where she focuses primarily on small firm outreach and employer development. Previously, she served as assistant director and associate director of career services at ASU for four years, providing student counseling services and program development. Ms. Williams graduated from Chicago-Kent College of Law in 2003, and has also worked as an associate attorney at large and small firms.

ACKNOWLEDGEMENTS

I am grateful to all the law students and new attorneys I've had the privilege to work with and learn from over the past decade, and especially to my colleagues in the General Practice, Solo and Small Firm Section of The Florida Bar. They have shared their experiences and offered insight into what it takes to succeed in the practice of law. It is with much love that I dedicate my work to my family, who has always believed in me, including those who have passed before me, and to those who continue each day to remind me to live in the moment with gratitude and joy. —LCH

My contribution to this book would not have been possible without the support of my colleagues in the career services office at the Sandra Day O'Connor College of Law at ASU, who continually raise the bar of hard work and professionalism. I am also especially grateful to my friends and family as a never ending source of enthusiasm and encouragement. This book is also dedicated to my husband Paul; his genuine respect and heartfelt support has made me feel like I can do it all. —SW

INTRODUCTION

This book was written to answer specific questions, such as...

Why consider small firm practice?
Where are the small firm jobs?
Why do I need to know about the business of practicing law?
How do I go about networking effectively with small firms?
What should I expect as a starting salary, and how do I go about negotiating?
What are core competencies, and why are they so critical to my small firm
  job search?
What steps do I need to take to succeed in my new position?

Our decision to undertake this project was based on several important factors:

Smaller law firms represent an often-minimized but vital employment segment for large numbers of law schools, job seekers, and new attorneys... AND there is a scarcity of good current information and resources about how to tap into this job market. And the third factor underlining the need for this book: the radical changes in the legal job market. Law graduates face the worst job market since the mid-1990's (projected to continue for several more years)...the restructuring of the Biglaw business model...the drastic reduction in Biglaw summer associate and entry-level hiring...and government agencies at all levels are confronted with hiring freezes and severe budgetary shortfalls.

Amid the gloom, though, an interesting phenomenon has occurred: the percentage of those getting jobs with small firms continues to rise at a significant rate.

Over the course of our respective legal careers, we both developed a passion for sharing our expertise about small firm practice. And while working together on a presentation, we were convinced that a book filled with practical information and advice would bridge the gap between the growing small firm market AND the candidates who seek the positions.

Our review of the literature reveals there are few books (and no recent publications) on how to help law students find work in an area that seemed to be actually hiring. What is available is fairly fractured: a column or Web posting here, a blog post there; everything ranging from general networking advice to some innocuous statements about how "different" small firms were compared to their larger brethren. More important than anything, this book seeks to connect the "what" with the "how." It provides the tools to act, whether you are a law student, a new grad, a junior associate, or a career development counselor.

In today's market, it is imperative that you as a job seeker not only utilize resources that describe the milieu, but also engage you purposefully in the process. To that end, we share perspectives and wisdom from multiple voices: law students, newer attorneys, and seasoned professionals. These individuals have either found jobs with small firms or have hired people to work in their firms. We also share timely tips, rookie mistakes, and reflective exercises to help you individualize the materials presented.

This book will walk you through a do-able venture. You will not only learn about the dynamics of small firm practice, and how to position yourself as an ideal candidate, but you will experience the highest reward when you engage in professional development practices that lead to your landing and succeeding in your new position.

—Linda Calvert Hanson, Esq., Samantha Williams, Esq., August, 2012

CHAPTER 1

Small Firms Are a Big Employer

As everyone would agree, the legal job market landscape is looking very different these days.

In just a few short years, in response to a deep recession and other economic forces...

Larger law firms downsized by nearly 9,500 lawyers.

A sizeable number of firms merged, splintered, or closed altogether.

Summer associate programs and entry-level hiring at larger law firms was all but eliminated in most firms, and has been slow to rebound.

The number of law school grads able to enter the legal workforce declined sharply.

Federal agencies and state governments experienced widespread hiring freezes.

As we all know from the mainstream media and legal blogosphere, substantial legal restructuring has resulted in uncounted rescinded job offers, slower hiring, and higher underemployment and unemployment rates for law students and recent graduates. But the upside—and, yes, there is an upside—the pain and wide-scale legal restructuring among larger firms has NOT been the same for small to midsized law firms. In fact, *smaller firms are the largest and fastest growing sector of the legal community, and more attorneys are currently working in firms with 50 or fewer attorneys than in any other legal employment segment.* And contrary to law school mythology, you and a significant number of your fellow graduates will begin your law careers in a smaller law firm. Because even in our gloomy economy, the truth is that small firms are providing a rich hiring opportunity for those who understand the dynamics of smaller firm practice, and who have prepared themselves to land the job.

Want some numbers to support this?

According to the National Association for Legal Career Professionals (NALP), almost half of the Class of 2011's 17,648 law grads employed in private practice was working in firms with fewer than 10 attorneys. And when you factor in midsized firms (26–50 attorneys), the percentage rises to nearly 60 percent! What's more, the Class of 2009 and 2010 showed an eight percent increase in the number of graduates who got their start with smaller firms. Not that employment opportunities at smaller firms are all that secret, of course: according to a recent survey by the ABA's General Practice Solo and Small Firm Division, 86 percent of more than 145,000 law students now expect to jump-start their legal career in smaller firms.

Clearly, smaller law firms represent a substantial employment market for entry-level lawyers in private practice. But it's not enough to want to get on board. You have to show you're ready.

We believe this book will provide the latest tools to help you find gainful employment with a small to midsized law firm, and to succeed in that practice. It will equip you with a working knowledge of the small firm model (which happens to be very different than in Biglaw), and it will provide concrete, tangible, practical steps to not only identify where the jobs are, but to get hired, and do what you've been educated to do: practice law.

At this point you might be thinking, *"Wow! Small firms are the answer! Sign me up."*

OK, but we need to take a breath, and acknowledge one important fact: smaller firms have not been immune from the Great Recession. Like many other small businesses facing decreasing revenues, small law firms have also been required to lay off staff (including attorneys), and some were even forced to close their doors. And yet, statistics tell us that smaller firms are still the really BIG legal employers across the nation! And before you finish this book, you will learn not only why this is true, but how you can take advantage of the wealth of employment opportunities this segment of the market can provide.

CHAPTER 2

Where the Jobs Are

Whether you follow mainstream media (*New York Times, Wall Street Journal*), or law blogs (*AbovetheLaw.com*, etc.), the story of the legal job market might lead you to generalize that all firms have been hit hard by great recession. That's not entirely accurate. More often than not, the stories refer to what is happening to the largest law firms in the largest US cities.

The truth is that law firm composition and hiring trends within most states varies a great deal—sometimes dramatically—from what is portrayed in the media because the economic impact on smaller firms is rarely headline material. The fact is, small firm employment opportunities are all around you, whether you live in the largest of cities or in a rural small town. And since the authors of this book are involved in small firm outreach in their home states, these two examples from the Southeast and Southwest show why law grads are looking to smaller firms to jump-start their careers:

Example #1: Florida. The state of Florida has nearly 65,000 "resident and actively licensed" attorneys, the fourth largest lawyer population in the US. According to The Florida Bar, of those surveyed, more than 75 percent work in firms of 10 or fewer lawyers (a figure that rises to 88 percent when you factor in firms of fewer than 25). Statistics show that of the more than half of the Class of 2010's 2,101 law grads who were hired by a Florida law firm, more than half of them began working in a firm of 10 or fewer attorneys. And while the largest concentration of law firms was in Miami/Ft. Lauderdale, the true mecca for entry-level lawyers was in Florida's medium-sized cities (e.g., Tampa Bay, Jacksonville, Orlando, etc.), which represent about 85 percent of the state's geographic area.

Example #2: Arizona. The state of Arizona has nearly 17,000 actively licensed attorneys. Nearly half of them are in private practice in firms of 2 to 49 attorneys, and a large percentage of them (nearly 30 percent) are solo practitioners. Not surprising, the great majority of Arizona's attorneys (74 percent) practice in Maricopa County (Phoenix). But if new lawyers assumed from these figures that they should focus their job-search efforts on Maricopa County, they would miss out on the significant pool of potential employers in some of Arizona's attractive but smaller cities, such as Tucson, Flagstaff, Prescott, and Yuma.

From both these examples, the takeaway is that by looking critically at the lawyer demographics within your target state, you are certain to discover pockets of small firm opportunities often overlooked by other job-seekers.

A Regional Snapshot

In the chart below, all states except New York and the District of Columbia reported that one-third or more of the law firm jobs were taken at small firms of 2 to 10 lawyers, and 29 states (particularly in the Southeast and New England) reported that more than two-thirds of the law firm jobs were taken at firms with fewer than 25 attorneys.

Here are a few additional examples from the chart:

- Five Midwest states and four Southeast states reported that 70 percent or more of the law firm jobs occurred in firms of 2 to 10.
- The West/Rocky Mountain region showed nine states with over 65 percent of their law firm jobs being in firms of 2 to 10.
- Forty-one percent of the law firm jobs taken in Pennsylvania were obtained in Philadelphia, which means that 59 percent were taken in smaller cities throughout the state. And of all of the recent graduates employed in law firms outside of Philadelphia, nearly half were employed in firms of fewer than 25 attorneys. *So, while smaller law firms positions had a solid presence within Philadelphia, the number of smaller firm positions taken in cities throughout the rest of the state was even stronger.*

It must be pointed out, however, that in California, Florida, Illinois, New York, and Texas—the five largest states listing more than 1,000 law firm jobs—there was no evident pattern of an increase in small firm hiring. Trends aside, though, it does appear that based upon the geographic distribution of smaller firm jobs obtained by the Class of 2010 graduates, there are significant opportunities for small firm employment in cities across the country, especially when you look beyond a state's largest metropolitan areas:

EMPLOYMENT FOR CLASS OF 2010 GRADUATES*

Region	State	City	Total law firm jobs taken in state/city	% of jobs in firms of 2-10	% of jobs in firms of 11-25
Northeast	CT		131	45.8%	16.0%
	MA		573	34.7%	6.1%
		Boston	387	19.9%	5.7%
	ME		32	53.1%	12.5%
	NH		33	51.5%	12.1%
	NJ		287	49.1%	9.1%
	NY		3,042	21.7%	5.0%
	NYC		2,396	11.3%	3.3%
	PA		591	37.6%	12.2%
	RI		48	54.2%	8.3%
	VT		18	77.8%	5.6%
Mid-Atlantic	DC		806	8.7%	2.1%
	DE		59	32.2%	10.2%
	MD		229	64.2%	8.3%
		Baltimore	91	51.6%	6.6%
	PN		591	37.6%	12.2%
		Philadelphia	231	23.4%	13.9%
	VA		307	48.2%	14.7%
Midwest	IA		101	67.3%	14.9%
	IL		1,046	38.7%	8.8%
		Chicago	809	30.4%	8.2%
	IN		224	44.6%	18.3%
	KS		93	62.4%	11.8%
	MI		379	41.2%	9.8%
	MN		299	43.8%	9.0%
		Mpls/St. Paul	188	28.2%	10.6%
	MO		246	33.3%	11.8%
	NE		111	64.9%	10.8%
	ND		33	60.6%	18.2%
	OH		512	44.9%	11.1%
		Cleveland	121	28.9%	11.6%
		Columbus	96	49.0%	11.5%
	SD		20	65.0%	16.0%
	WI		228	52.2%	9.6%

(continued next page)

Region	State	City	Total law firm jobs taken in state/city	% of jobs in firms of 2-10	% of jobs in firms of 11-25
Southeast	AL		185	35.7%	7.6%
	AR		89	69.7%	15.7%
	FL		1,777	50.0%	12.1%
		Miami	244	37.3%	14.3%
	GA		488	45.1%	8.6%
		Atlanta	290	32.8%	6.9%
	KY		159	57.2%	13.8%
	LA		308	45.8%	20.1%
		New Orleans	133	33.1%	21.1%
	MS		103	48.5%	8.7%
	OK		184	60.9%	13.0%
	NC		325	55.1%	4.6%
	SC		134	62.7%	8.2%
	TN		213	44.1%	12.2%
	TX		1,316	41.6%	10.6%
		Austin	114	43.9%	12.3%
		Dallas	275	28.0%	6.5%
		Houston	479	35.5%	13.4%
	WV		96	38.5%	5.2%
West/Rocky Mt.	AK		16	62.5%	6.3%
	AZ		202	56.4%	9.9%
	CA		2,301	37.1%	7.7%
		Los Angeles	563	22.2%	7.1%
		San Diego	270	47.0%	6.3%
		San Francisco	317	24.6%	7.3%
	CO		217	43.3%	14.7%
		Denver	131	32.8%	14.5%
	ID		44	59.1%	9.1%
	HA		28	35.7%	17.9%
	MT		33	45.5%	27.3%
	NM		69	62.3%	13.0%
	NV		129	46.5%	10.9%
	OR		154	55.2%	9.7%
	UT		151	56.3%	10.6%
	WA		307	55.7%	5.5%
		Seattle	192	45.8%	4.7%
	WY		28	75.0%	14.3%

*JD's AND JOBS 2011, PUBLISHED BY THE NATIONAL ASSOCIATION FOR LEGAL CAREER PROFESSIONALS

CHAPTER 3

Nine Reasons to Start at a Small Firm

New attorneys working in smaller firms are quick to list the advantages, especially when compared to classmates who joined the ranks of Biglaw.

What are those advantages?

Generally, small firm practice offers young associates greater responsibility and an accelerated, hands-on case experiences. This is a huge plus because new law graduates are eager to immediately delve into the practice of law. So, first on their list of priorities is to not be relegated to a windowless corner, churning out legal research and writing projects, or performing document reviews for the first year or two. This ability for a new small firm attorney to gain "front-line" rather than "library" time long before a similarly junior associate would experience in the large firm is paramount to most.

Nine advantages to small firm practice
- More hands-on responsibility sooner
- Full case management and greater autonomy
- More immediate client contact
- Greater personal interaction with a larger subset of people
- Ability to see first-hand how your work helps others
- More collegial, family-like atmosphere
- Greater flexibility and other quality of life distinctions
- More integral involvement in firm decisions sooner
- Potential to develop a new area of specialization as expertise evolves

Joseph D. McAllister, a third-year associate in Salt Lake City, shared his thoughts about small firm practice:

"I love the freedom and autonomy. From the start, I have been doing substantive legal work. I sat second-chair on a seven-day civil trial after six months,

and after a year was first chair for a two-day civil trial. I argued in front of the Court of Appeals during my first year, and have argued countless dispositive motions. I also have the chance to represent our clients at mediations and arbitrations, and in more informal negotiation and settlement meetings. What I love about my job is the chance to get down in the trenches, and actually confront and solve legal problems."

In smaller firms, cases are more typically worked by one or two attorneys at the most, as opposed to a team of large firm lawyers who would each handle a piece, or different aspect, of the case. The smaller firm approach results in a more complete understanding of the intricacies of handling a case and full case management responsibility much sooner for the smaller firm associate. Amy Bokor, a fifth-year associate in Charlotte, NC, shared her experience:

"…I have opportunities to enhance my practice in ways that my peers at larger firms have not. While they're stuck doing legal research projects (which I have had plenty of as well), I've been able to handle my own cases, go through trials, mediations, depositions, and arbitrations. I get to be on the front-line rather than in the library."

Besides more immediate client contact, another often cited advantage to small firm practice is the opportunity to enjoy greater personal interaction with a larger subset of people, including lawyers in other firms, mediators, court personnel, and witnesses. And, just as important, there is the chance to see first-hand how your participation at the firm helps clients with family law matters, bankruptcy, real estate closings, estate planning, and cases involving more personal interactions, as opposed to the large business transactions typical of Biglaw.

Still other advantages cited by small firm attorneys include a more collegial work environment, in which you get to know everyone in your office. This usually allows for greater flexibility and other quality of life distinctions. Amy Bokor says that working at a small firm practice gave her flexibility in parenting. *"After the birth of my son,"* she says, *"My priorities changed, and I needed the flexibility to have 'mommy time'. My firm allowed me to work four days and change my office hours so I could get home before afternoon traffic."*

Other aspects of small firm life were cited by Kelly, a fourth-year associate in a 15-attorney Atlanta employment firm. *"I enjoy the collegial atmosphere, the sophisticated work, and the number of opportunities early on,"* she said. *"I also appreciate that my job is separate from my life, and [that at my firm] we do not have mandatory social functions or recruiting requirements. I'm able to come to work, work very hard, be rewarded for my successes, and leave work behind me at the end of the day."*

And there are still other advantages to small firm practice.

It's less competitive than life in big firms; there is an opportunity to be more integrally involved in firm decisions once you establish yourself at the firm; and there is the chance to develop new areas of specialization within the firm once you establish competency and a readiness to draw in a fresh client base (this alone is an opportunity that would be hard to replicate within the complexity and structure of a large firm). In all, new lawyers in small firm practice report at least nine advantages over classmates working in larger firms.

One more advantage: the practical legal skills and experiences you gain sooner in smaller firms will enhance your marketability if and when you wish to explore other markets later.

Seven (possible) disadvantages to small firm practice

Small firm practice isn't for everyone, of course; it's not a panacea. It comes with its own challenges, its own distinctions. For example:

- Small firms may be perceived as less prestigious
- Small firms are less able to offer high-end benefits
- Small firms have fewer resources and staff support
- Small firms have lesser starting salaries
- Small firms usually lack a formal training program
- For candidates, the job "fit" is more critical
- Finding and landing a position takes more time

And five more...

- Small firms are usually not located at the most prestigious addresses
- Small firms are usually not located at the top of high-rise buildings
- Small firms are usually not set in opulent surroundings with in-house gyms, courier service, and weekly deliveries of fresh flowers.
- Small firms usually don't offer club memberships, or the opportunity to attend CLE's in the Bahamas.
- Smaller firms have fewer support staff, so you may be expected to do more of your own administrative work. And since "fit" is more critical to success and happiness in the smaller firm, if you do not get along with everyone on your team, there is no transferring to another floor. Your option usually is to leave and find another job.

But for some, the more significant distinction concerns salary. A small firm's base starting salary invariably is less than that paid by large firms, although it is worth noting that NALP's Associate Salaries Survey reports that after five years of practice there is a diminishing gap between large and small firms.

A new lawyer needs to put all these factors into perspective. For example, a small firm may not be able to start you at a handsome salary, but the trade-off is that you may get to work fewer hours, and the compensation plan may be more flexible and creative. This more flexible plan could include financial incentives for bringing in new clients, or variable compensation based upon the client fee, or, as Amy Bokor mentioned earlier, you might warrant a more flexible working arrangement after several years of demonstrating competency and commitment to the firm. Another important distinction between SmallLaw and Biglaw is the lack of a formal training program. Smaller law firms more often have an on-the-job-learn-as-you-go training model. Some newer practitioners see this as a disadvantage; others enjoy being able to accept responsibility at their own pace.

Regardless of the differing perspectives, the universal challenge to smaller firm practice is this: how to find a position and how to get hired in the new legal economy, topics for which we have dedicated several chapters to help you succeed.

IN THEIR OWN WORDS

Q: What do you enjoy about small firm practice?

"I enjoy the more casual environment. Every partner has an open door policy here, and it never feels like a factory. I think a smaller firm gives a young associate a better opportunity to work side-by-side with experienced lawyers."
—Lisa (Class of 2008)

"I enjoy the collegial atmosphere, the sophisticated work, and the number of opportunities presented early on. I also appreciate that my job is separate from my life. We don't have mandatory social functions or recruiting requirements. I am able to come to work, work very hard and be rewarded for my successes, and [get to] leave work behind at the end of the day."—Kelly (Class of 2007)

"[What I enjoy] is the ability and responsibility to work most aspects of a case from the start." —Troy (Class of 2010)

"[What I appreciate] is the flexibility to be a mom and an attorney. In addition, I have opportunities to enhance my practice in ways that my peers at larger firms have not. While they're stuck doing legal research projects (which I have had plenty of as well), I've been able to handle my own cases, go through trials, mediations, depositions, and arbitrations. I get to be on the front-line rather than in the library." —Amy (Class of 2006)

"[I enjoy] the freedom and autonomy. We do not spend our time drafting research memos or toiling on some meaningless document review. From the start, I have been doing substantive legal work. After just six months, I sat second-chair on a seven-day civil trial. After a year, I was first-chair for a two-day day civil trial, I argued before the Court of Appeals, and have argued countless dispositive motions. I also have the chance to represent our clients at mediations and arbitrations, and in more informal negotiation and settlement meetings. What I love about my job is the chance to get down in the trenches and actually confront and solve legal problems." —Joseph (Class of 2007)

"Although we have a billable requirement, I am able to make it home around 6 every day, and work only a few hours on the weekend." —Nikki (Class of 2009)

"[What I enjoy is that we're] more of a close knit group, and I have more flexibility and a better work/life balance." —Shelly (Class of 2007)

"While we enjoy the benefits of a large firm's resources (unified billing, legal research resources, referral of business, etc.), we [also] have camaraderie in our office." —Adam (Class of 2006)

"I get to work in a variety of projects instead of being restricted to a focused area of law. For example, I get to practice both patent prosecution and patent litigation instead of just one or the other." —Rick (Class of 2008)

"I am responsible for my own case load. I work completely independently on each case from start to finish. I don't have billable hours."
—Kathryn (Class of 2010)

CHAPTER 4

How Small Firms and Biglaw Differ

Law students often assume that the practice of law is the same at all private firms regardless of size. It isn't, and how well you understand that could make all the difference in your getting hired.

No doubt you're most familiar with large firms because of their visibility during the on-campus interview process. Then there are all those exciting stories of summer associates who got to work in high-rise law offices, and enjoyed lavish restaurant meals at the firm's expense. The experience of small firm practice is starkly *different*…in many ways. And while it's always helpful to be knowledgeable about any potential employer, it is particularly true of the nuances and dynamics of small firms; not only how they practice law, but also their hiring needs. It is to your advantage to learn as much as you can so you can incorporate that into an effective job search. Because when it comes to the small firm job search, knowledge is power…and *that* could translate into a job offer.

Types of Small Firms

The general practice firm. The general practice firm handles a wide variety of cases and is staffed with a "jack-and-jill-of-all-trades" type of lawyer. Such firms offer a broad range of services from civil litigation and commercial contracts to criminal defense, and they generally take anything that walks through the door. This type of firm tends to handle less complex matters than Biglaw because they are less able to staff larger cases. The experience gained at these smaller firms is indicative of the practice itself; broad practice-area coverage, and an immediate opportunity to interact with clients and to make decisions regarding cases. This type of firm is especially appealing to law students who are unsure of what area of practice to follow, and who are seeking variety in their work. That said, though, true general practitioners are becoming less common in major cities, and are mainly found in more rural communities that have fewer lawyers.

The specialty, or boutique, firm. These firms handle only matters that pertain to a discrete practice area, such as labor law or intellectual property. Specialty, or boutique, firms represent a growing trend in the legal community, mainly because it is difficult to be all things to all clients. In addition, this model tends to be more fiscally attractive because the attorneys who specialize in a particular area can charge a higher rate per billable hour. If you intend to specialize in one type of practice area, it makes sense to concentrate your job search efforts on this type of firm.

The complementary practices firm. By far, the greatest number of small law firms falls within the complementary practices model. In this model, several supporting (complementary) practice areas are handled by different attorneys so the firm doesn't have to outsource its services to meet the needs of clients. Example: one of the firm's lawyers might specialize in criminal defense, another in family law, and a third in estates and trusts. In such a firm, it might bring together the attorney who focuses on creditor rights with another who specializes in business formations, and yet another who practices commercial real estate. Partners in complementary practices prefer to keep things in-house, and not risk losing future business by referring long-standing clients to another firm.

What Sets Smaller Firms Apart?

Smaller firms are typically staffed with lawyers with broad skill-sets who are less dependent on specific industries that "crash and burn." This explains why lawyers who focused on real estate transactions ran into trouble in the collapse of the national housing market. The lesson here is that small firm lawyers with varied practices are able to morph into different areas if one of those areas no longer supports a particular client base. For example: suppose a small firm whose practice involves corporate leases, business formations, and wills and trusts, experiences a significant drop in corporate lease work. Even though a third of the firm's total billable hours have been lost, it would still have a diversified practice. The firm would ramp up its wills and trusts work, and make it an even larger part of their portfolio.

Small firms tend to survive in weak economies. They have lower overhead (so they're usually not overstaffed when the volume of work erodes), and they tend to grow at slower rates than large firms. Small firms are also generally able to adapt more quickly and effectively to client needs because policy decisions—such a negotiating alternative fee arrangements—do not have to be considered and decided upon by one or more committees as in large firms.

The business practice mind-set. At smaller firms, every person—from law clerk and associate on up—must pull his or her own weight. The work is much more visible than at a large firm, and unproductive lawyers become obvious very quickly as opposed to large firm lawyers who might be able to hide their lack of productivity for a longer period of time. To survive, a small firm practice must be more entrepreneurial, and everyone is expected to begin rainmaking from day one. Out of necessity, small firms have a business practice mind-set because every hour that is not a billable hour comes out of their own pocket.

The ability to weather the storm. If profits drop significantly, a law firm must tap into its capital reserves; if profits continue to fall, the capital reserves are endangered, and the firm must implement layoffs and other cost-cutting measures. This is all pretty familiar during these times of Biglaw restructuring as firms scramble to respond to the client-driven buyers' market. Of course, all law firms feel the effects of an economic downturn…but small and mid-sized law firms are usually better at weathering the storm. Why? They usually don't have high overhead; that is, the fixed monthly costs—rent, staff salaries, utility bills, etc.—that must be paid each month regardless of whether they generate $1,000 or $100,000 in fees. And small firms are very cost-conscious. For example, their offices are typically located outside high-rent, downtown areas. As a result, they're able to charge significantly lower billable rates, which translates into a greater likelihood of obtaining and retaining clients. In fact, the current economic downturn has caused many downsized Biglaw attorneys to set up their own solo or small firms so they can charge lower billable hour rates and satisfy their client's demands.

Small firm lawyers wear many hats. By definition, small firms have fewer attorneys, so the opportunity to delegate tasks is limited. For example, the small firm attorney is not only the legal advocate (drafting the complaint), but he or she might also be the courier (delivering and filing said complaint to the courthouse), and the litigator arguing the case. In addition, small firm attorneys often must act as their own problem-solver because—unlike Biglaw—there aren't many colleagues down the hall with whom to consult when a complex issue arises. And because small firms don't typically have a large support staff and administrative personnel, the attorneys must also handle marketing, rainmaking, payroll, and human resource matters.

The roles taken on by small firm attorneys are often dictated by their clientele and practice areas. Clients of small firms tend to be individuals and small companies who are also usually located in the same city, and possibly the same neighborhood as the firm. Because these attorneys tend to have more personal interaction with their clients, they must also sometimes act as a counselor who listens and offers guidance as opposed to strictly legal advice. This is often true in such areas as family law and criminal defense. Before you begin your small firm job search, it is incredibly important to fully appreciate all the hats worn by small firm attorneys.

The new employee: will he/she fit? The notion of "fit" goes to the culture, or the "feel," of the law firm. It is not something to be treated lightly.

Whether you "fit" or not will have a tremendous impact on whether you would be happy at the firm. After all, you would be spending 50 to 80 hours a week—half your waking life—with colleagues and supervisors. And if you disliked those around you (or they, you), it would be difficult to motivate yourself to go to work every day. The notion of "fit" is also tied to one's personality type, personal values, and communications style. If you're a more gregarious, extraverted type who thrives in an active environment, you need to consider how well would you fit in a more laid-back firm; conversely, if you're more introverted, consider how well would you fit in more active, extraverted environment. While we're at it, ask yourself whether you place the same amount of importance on community service as the attorneys in the firm where you want to work: is the firm one of the stuffy "white shoe" firms, or is the firm culture more laid-back, where no one wears a suit unless he or she is going to court?

"Hiring a new employee is a big deal for a small law firm," says Kirk Kirkconnell, founding partner of a five-attorney criminal defense firm in Orlando FL, *"A new person in small office affects everyone else in the firm more profoundly and directly than in a larger firm with more people. It's like adding a drop of food coloring in a glass versus a swimming pool."*

Another small firm attorney put it this way:

"We see resumes all the time from well-educated, well-qualified attorneys and law students. But my office only has four employees—five if you include my assistant—and I can't risk bringing someone else in who doesn't get along with everyone." Eric Robinson, a 2010 graduate of the Sandra Day O'Connor College of Law at Arizona State University, agrees. *"Small firms,"* he says, *"Know that you're qualified. But what they want is someone they feel comfortable with; someone they*

feel comfortable introducing to clients, and who they can go to lunch with during the week. It's important to small firms to establish the relationship first. Chemistry is very important."

In short, small firms are keenly aware of the notion of "fitness" when considering bringing someone into their group. After all, if the new lawyer doesn't get along with colleagues, there is no moving them to the 12th floor.

How to Identify a Firm's Culture

Law firm Web sites are a great place to start learning about a firm's culture. There you can discover specific information that you can use in your job search, such as:

- How active are the attorneys within the community? Attorneys who actively participate in local non-profit organizations understand that giving back to the community is important. They also realize that community involvement is essential for meeting and bringing in new clients. Many attorneys serve on the Board of Directors for non-profit organizations like the Foundation for Blind Children, Homeward Bound, and Habitat for Humanity. You might be pleasantly surprised to learn that you and the attorney have both volunteered for the same organization!
- Are firm members active in any professional organizations like local bar associations or relevant trade groups? Attorneys who are active in the community understand the importance of networking, and will probably expect new-hires to share that same value.
- Did the attorneys come from different parts of the country or from one particular region? This can give you some insight in terms of who they might favor as an applicant. Pay particular attention to where hiring partners attended law school because you will have an edge with someone who attended your current school or alma mater.
- How active are newer associates in terms of actually practicing law? Do their profiles indicate they are practicing generally in areas like commercial litigation, or are they focusing on specific areas like employment and health law?

Studying the firm's Web site can also help you determine:

- How long the firm has been in existence.
- Does the firm have a clear political bent? If you're a staunch conservative, you probably won't fit in well at a firm whose attorneys all come directly from the ACLU. And if diversity is important to you, you'll want to check

whether there are any women, minorities, or gays and lesbians who are in positions of authority.

- ***What is the firm's Partner/Associate ratio?*** If you will be the only law clerk or associate in a firm comprised only of partners, you should be diligent in trying to get enough guidance and supervision. Also keep in mind how you relate to your superiors. Do you prefer to report to just one person such as a supervisor, or would you rather receive assignments from a variety of attorneys?

- ***Is the firm local or does it also have a national presence?*** Does it have offices located across the country or within a specific region? Firms with offices solely on the East Coast may be more conservative those on the West Coast. If you love the culture and the mind-set of a city like Chicago, you may find that you fit in well with law firms there.

- ***What is the firm's client mix?*** A firm's client list can provide valuable insight into a firm's culture. Find out whether the firm has only a few really big clients or a broad mix. Fewer (but larger) clients can signify a conservative policy, and might raise a warning flag for you as a job applicant if the firm lost its big client. A more diverse client base could indicate a more liberal and growth-oriented type of culture.

After completing your research, ask yourself if you could be happy in a particular firm if you had to spend 10 hours or more there Monday through Friday (with the occasional Saturday, of course). What if the firm's partners all are your grandfather's age? Would you feel comfortable in an environment with such a large generation gap? Do you share the firm's approach to "collaborative" divorce? How would you feel working for a firm full of good ol' boys? Would it be distracting to see the named partner walk around in his socks all day?

CHAPTER 5

The Recruiting & Hiring Cycle

The unpredictable nature of small firm hiring tends to frustrate job-seekers.

Candidates are accustomed to applying to firms that participate in OCI, the on-campus interview process that occurs in the fall and spring of the academic year. However, the vast majority of firms that participate in fall OCI are large law firms. And large firms hire based on perceived need while smaller law firms hire based on *actual need*. In fact, smaller firms usually don't know what their hiring needs are going to be next quarter, much less next year. So, when smaller firms do hire, it usually happens unexpectedly (when a law clerk abruptly quits her job to participate in a clinic next semester, or an associate resigns to go work for the county Public Defender, or when client business at the small firm suddenly picks up so much that the firm needs to hire someone to cover the extra work). Of course, some small and midsized firms do hire through OCI, but it is almost always in the spring. Such firms tend to be in the major metropolitan areas, and to some degree can anticipate their workload for the upcoming summer months when there is a pool of law students from which to choose.

Many law school career services offices do a great job of recruiting small firms to OCI. So, before you begin your outreach, make sure you know exactly which of your target firms will be recruiting on campus. Be sure to schedule an appointment with your career counselor, who is likely to have insights into local bar organizations that support small firms, have connections to certain attorneys who are active in the community, and who can provide you with a copy of the local bar directory.

> **Note:** it helps if your career services office knows that you are actively seeking work with smaller firms so you can be notified when those opportunities arise.

Recruiting

Unlike Biglaw, small firms do not usually have structured summer associate programs. So, don't expect any of the usual summer associate perks such as expensive lunches and out-of-town retreats. When a small firm hires a student for the summer, it is usually because there is a need at that particular time. Nor are summer associates as likely to get an offer for post-graduate employment at the end of the summer because the firm can't anticipate staff needs that far in advance. It's more likely that you will be asked to get in touch with the firm the following year, either upon graduation or after you pass the Bar (assuming, of course, you do a great job as a clerk).

Hiring

When it comes to hiring lateral attorneys ("laterals") and summer associates, the large firms usually involve multiple levels of bureaucracy. Hiring committees usually consist of a Recruiting Manager, Hiring Partner, other Partners, and even Senior Associates. And the committee members analyze and discuss each candidate's qualifications, and make decisions based on a screening of resumes, interviews, and call-backs. By contrast, the small firm hiring process is usually more streamlined and less formal. When an especially promising resume arrives at the firm, the initial conversation between partners might go something like this: *"Hey, Laura, do you want to take a look at the student resume that came in the mail today? It looks really good, and I know you need some help with discovery on that big case you just landed."*

Small firms usually hire only after licensure. Often law students are frustrated by their small firm job search because there is an expectation that students get jobs *prior* to graduation. It isn't always true. In fact, for very small firms of 2 to 10 lawyers—which accounts for more than a third of all private practice jobs—nearly half the jobs are obtained *after* graduation. That's because the busy nature of small firm practice requires full and complete utilization of every lawyer in the firm to cover trials and hearings, take depositions, and sign court documents (none of which new grads can do until after they've passed the Bar). This would seem obvious, but it's a reality that most students and new grads overlook. In fact, small firms simply don't have the same ability as Biglaw to pay someone to just do research and writing. But just because smaller firms usually hire only after licensure doesn't mean you should postpone your small firm job search. There are smaller firms out there that do hire law students as clerks in anticipation of becoming licensed. In fact, the period between taking the Bar and learning the results is a great time for both parties to see if the working relationship should continue after the clerk becomes licensed. It's also a prime opportunity for the clerk to show the attorney how much value he/she adds to the firm. But even if the firm is not in a position to hire you as a law clerk, many candidates have been able to position themselves in such a way that the firm's partner will say, *"We think you're really great, so please come back to us as soon as you have your Bar number."*

Small firms usually don't post open positions. It may seem counter-intuitive, but most small firm positions are never advertised. This is a frustration for law students and new attorneys accustomed to applying to jobs posted online or through their career services office. However, the fact that small firms very rarely post jobs makes more sense when you appreciate that there is a significant cost involved with the hiring process. Not only can it cost several hundreds of dollars to post a job, but the time required to hire a new employee is money lost because the hiring attorney(s) of a smaller firm cannot bill for that time.

Here is a rough breakdown of all the tasks that must be accomplished when a small firm seeks to hire a law clerk or a new associate:

- Draft the job description
- Post the job (after speaking with various career services offices and researching other appropriate job-posting sites like bar association Web sites, etc.)
- Receive, compile, and review resumes and cover letters
- Give careful thought which of the applicants seems most qualified, and who will be the best fit based on submitted materials
- Call applicants to schedule interviews
- Conduct interviews
- Collaborate/meet with staff members who met with candidates to gain feedback
- Make hiring decision

The hours spent assessing and interviewing candidates are hours not spent billing or spent with the hiring attorney's family. It is for these reasons that small firms only post open positions as a last resort. So, if small firms don't post jobs, how are these positions filled? The old-fashioned way, by word-of-mouth. Attorneys confer with one another all the time: as opposing counsel; as law committee members; at networking functions, CLE's, holiday parties, and so on. And it's by word-of-mouth, also, that approximately 75 percent of a small firm's caseload comes from attorney referrals. The point here is that it is less time-consuming for a small firm to post a job than it is for one of the attorneys to pick up the phone and ask for a recommendation from a colleague. It's a conversation that might goes something like this:

Q: *"Hi Joe, this is Maggie. Business is picking up and I can really use some help. Do you know any law students who would be interested in clerking 10 hours a week?"*

A: *"Yes, as a matter of fact, I just met one at the County Bar lunch yesterday. He's a 2L who's interested in learning more about civil litigation, and he seems really great. I have his resume in my inbox. I'll forward it to you."*

In this scenario, Maggie has just saved herself countless non-billable hours (and a huge expense) by picking up the phone. And since she also trusts Joe's judgment, she can be fairly confident that the student will be a good fit. Smaller firms that do post jobs will most often do so using free Web sites like Craigslist, trade-based listservs, and law school job banks. Be aware of where small firms typically post in your region, and check those sites regularly.

If a position is posted, it's usually for an immediate need. Other than firms who recruit during spring OCI, most small firms post jobs that begin right away. It may involve only 10 to 20 hours per week, but you must be prepared to begin working immediately. If you are unable to apply for a position because you are otherwise committed—if you're beginning to study for the Bar exam, or you're currently juggling class work, or clinical hours, or student organization commitments—it is better to contact the firm later, and ask them to keep you in mind for project work or when another position becomes available.

IN THEIR OWN WORDS

Q: What advice do you have for new lawyers looking for work?

A: Don't just send out a resume and hope for a call-back. Pound the pavement. Firm partners are busy, so follow-up even if you have to go visit them at their office. They know they need help, but you need to make sure you are there when they decide to hire someone." —Joseph (Class of 2007)

A: Network, network, network. Small and midsized firms don't hire as regularly as big law firms. The students who get hired usually know someone who works there." —Nikki (Class of 2009)

A: Be persistent. A small firm typically does not have an office manager. It's usually the managing partner who is also trying to keep his busy practice alive. [In fact], the firm might be so busy that it needs to hire another lawyer, but the current lawyers are all too busy to take the time to hire a new lawyer. Keep following up and be flexible in the interview schedule to accommodate the firm's needs."—AMY (CLASS OF 2006)

A: Do not be afraid to call friends, family, and other contacts to get referrals. Take attorneys out to lunch to ask advice and help in the process of looking for a job. Follow that up with a nice (handwritten) note thanking them for the time and advice. Make a list of people you know who may know an attorney. Try to get those individuals to call the attorney on your behalf. Follow up with the attorney as often as possible, and when you do land a job, send a thank you note to the attorney/contact informing them of your new job."—ADAM (CLASS OF 2006)

A: Network, network, network. And be aggressive when doing so. Unless you are in the top 5% or are connected, it can be difficult. Therefore, a student should get to know people while in school and utilize every networking opportunity. Once a contact is established, the key is to follow-up. There are a lot of good people in the legal community and they are easy to talk to. One only needs to make the effort. Also, [make use of] your career services office."—TROY (CLASS OF 2010)

A: With small firms, the most important factor is going to be where you live or where you are from. And they don't want to train someone who [they think] is going to leave in a couple of years."—KATHRYN (CLASS OF 2010)

A: If you want to join a small to midsized firm with a sophisticated practice, your best bet is to work at a larger, respected firm in the same area for a few years to gain the training and experience that big firms provide. It may sound counter-intuitive to suggest going to a big firm if you want to work at a smaller firm in the end. But in reality, most sophisticated small to midsize firms add associates through lateral hiring, and don't really hire first-year associates very often."—ANDREW (CLASS OF 2007)

SECTION II
JUMP-STARTING YOUR LEGAL CAREER

CHAPTER 6

Job Search Strategies

Smaller law firms tend to focus on a few complementary practice areas, which means new lawyers don't have the luxury of "trying out" a bunch of different practice areas to see what fits and what doesn't. How to find out what will fit and what won't?

Career self-assessment is an activity you must do, not just read about.

Career self-assessment can help steer you towards a career path in law that is closely aligned with your personality, your values, your psychological needs, your communication style, your motivated skills, and your career interests. You don't have to know exactly which area(s) of law you want to practice before looking for work, but not having any idea at all might lead potential employers to assume that you lack insight, or worse…that you are a bit of a flake. In fact, looking for work without doing any career self-assessment is an exercise in frustration. It's a little like landing in a strange city, and hoping to find your way without GPS or Google Maps. You'll do a lot of wandering, and hope that you get where you want to go.

Fortunately, undergraduate university and law school career offices are amply stocked with self-assessment tools to help you identify what your goals are, what you're interested in practicing, and what you hope to accomplish in the short- and long-term. And there is a wealth of self-assessment tools online; some are free, many others are inexpensive. The bottom line: career self-assessment is essential for any job-seeker…but it is an especially important component of your small firm job search. The ability to articulate your goals and objectives is not only an attractive trait in a potential candidate, but it gives a small firm employer a greater certainty about whether or not you would be a good fit.

How to Choose a Practice Area

How can you discover what's right for you? Here's a simple exercise:

Imagine your legal career as a giant ball containing every type of law imaginable. Your task is to add or remove the various practice areas based on your experience in and out of the classroom. *Do you like torts and contracts classes? Were you intrigued by a presentation on personal injury law? Did you dislike your experience with the environmental law clinic? How do you feel about patent work?* As you consider each of your classes, adding or removing different practice areas, your ball will begin to take shape around the areas of law that most appeal to you. As simple as this exercise seems, it can actually make you a more decisive, more attractive job candidate, and have the effect of guiding you towards a career you actually enjoy. On the other hand, failing to commit to a particular practice area is not a catastrophe although it can delay your ability to get a job. Many law students are afraid of committing because they "want to keep their options open." This strategy has its limitations, says former law career counselor Susan Gainen, owner of Pass the Baton, LLC:

> *"Keeping your options open as a primary career development tool has its limits. Yes, there are 31 flavors at* Baskin-Robbins, *but when you get to the front of the line and say, 'I want to keep my options open', the server will ask you to step aside. The person behind you may not be ready to commit to one flavor, but her willingness to explore Chocolate, Peanut, and Peppermint gets her an ice cream cone."*

Don't make the mistake of guessing what type of career is right for you! As you begin your search, you will increase your chances of getting hired if you remember this: Many small law firms simply do not have enough work to keep a new employee busy for 40 hours per week.

> **The bottom line:** making yourself available only as a *full-time* employee is like asking for steak when a burger and fries are the only things on the menu.

You're better off asking for project work. This means you are essentially a contract-based employee who is hired to work a set number of hours on a specific project. Perhaps it is to help them with researching or conducting document review for one particular case, or researching a topic for their upcoming CLE presentation. While it's not ideal, it is advantageous for several reasons: it fills in a few new lines on your resume, and, more importantly, it gets your foot in the door! Once you have a project under your belt (and they like your work product), it is more likely they will call you for other projects. Next thing you know, you're working steadily on a part-time or even full-time basis because the firm recognizes what value you bring. It happened just that way for Tyler Carroll, a 2010 law graduate from Arizona State University:

"…Most firms can use help in one form or another. What you'll probably see in the market is that people will get a job doing whatever firms need them to do. This can mean being a law clerk for four hours, for six hours, or even part time. But once you are there, it's up to you to make the most of the experience."

When to Start Looking

When it comes to the small firm job search, timing is everything.

That's no cliché; it's true.

As we said earlier, most small firms do not participate in structured OCI programs, and they hire only sporadically based on need. So, limiting your job search to the two times per year when on campus interviewing occurs mean you will most certainly miss out on a number of opportunities. Joseph McAllister, a small firm attorney in Salt Lake City, puts it this way:

"I tell every law student I know that if your job search begins and ends with OCI you are in big trouble!"

So when exactly should you start your search? Now, because…timing is everything. And the sooner you start identifying target firms and trying to make meaningful connections, the more likely it is that you will find a job. Those who start identifying target firms and trying to make meaningful connections early on will have the advantage.

You should also know this: the successful small firm search is not just a function of when, but how much time and effort you're willing to put into it. The process is a lot like making a capital investment; you put a lot of time into it on the front end so you're more likely to yield gain down the road. In fact, the most successful job seekers spend months doing research, attending networking functions, conducting informational interviews, etc., until one day they get The Call or The Interview. It happened just like that to one small firm attorney in Charlotte NC: *"I sent them my resume after I passed the North Carolina Bar,"* he said, *"And I just continued to follow up until I got an interview."*

Even if you are the perfect candidate, though, an initial "no" may be a factor of bad timing for that particular firm. So, don't take no for a "no". In fact, it's quite common for students and graduates to circle back *repeatedly* to the same small firm, and get an interview only after multiple contacts. It works like this: Say you meet a small firm attorney at a networking event in February, and you mention that you're looking for summer work. The attorney says he would like to help you but doesn't have any work at the moment. Two months pass, and you meet the attorney a second time when your student organization invites him to make a presentation. Another month passes. Now, it's

May, and the attorney—who didn't need any help back in February—lands a big case, and suddenly needs someone to research case law and draft the pleadings. Next thing you know, your phone rings. You get The Call because of your continued networking efforts.

As we said, timing is…well, you get the idea.

Where to Start Looking

Unfortunately, there is no one comprehensive information source for smaller firms like there is for large firms, such as NALP's *Directory of Legal Employers*. Smaller firms also do not typically use legal placement firms ("recruiters, head-hunters"), and many of them do not participate in OCI. Yet there are some steps to take that will help you decide where, and in what practice areas, you wish to practice:

Your best resource

People are the absolute best and the most current resource for identifying promising small firm employment prospects. And, of course, the individuals who are plugged into the legal community are your best sources: local attorneys and alumni, law professors, a courthouse bailiff or a judge's judicial assistant. With their help, you can learn a lot about the firms where you're applying. For example, ask them…

What is the firm's reputation within the community?
What area of law is the firm's primary focus, and what areas are they moving away from?
Is the firm experiencing growth or are they facing financial difficulties?

The most obvious resource at your disposal will be your law school career services office. The staff understands that smaller firms are where most graduates land their first job, and most career offices have outstanding resources at their disposal. In fact, some law schools have counselors specializing in the small firm market. If you haven't yet visited with your school's career counselor, put this book down and schedule your appointment.

Inside information

If you want inside information, get to know the ex-classmates and former colleagues who work for small firms. What they know could provide job or project opportunities before they're generally known. For example, one of your ex-classmates or colleagues might mention that she is not staying on for the fall semester, which could mean a prime opportunity to take her place. In fact, one hiring tactic that small firms use is to ask outgoing clerks for referrals and recommendations so they can avoid going through the hiring process again. The same goes for colleagues at large firms, from whom you might learn that a couple of their attorneys are planning to jump ship to set up their own partnership. All you need to do is check your local bar association membership directory to see when they update their contact information to that of the new firm, and then get in touch with them ASAP.

Legal recruiters

For some law students and recent graduates, the idea of using a legal recruiter (headhunter) seems like a no-brainer. After all, it's easy, convenient, and they do all the work for you without cost, don't they? Well, before you start speed-dialing legal recruiters in your area, here are the facts:

- Legal recruiters tend to work with Am Law 100 and 200 firms, and/or high-end specialty boutiques or very prestigious smaller firms. Many of them will also only work with licensed practitioners with two to six years of experience. Still, it's not a bad idea for you to begin developing a relationship with a recruiter early on. A good recruiter will at least talk to recent graduates and offer job market advice, networking strategies, and how to make good career decisions.
- Smaller firms *rarely* use recruiters because of the expense (the industry average is about 25 percent of the base salary of the attorney placed at the firm). If you calculate the fee for placing someone into a position with a $60,000 annual salary, it works out to $15,000. This is a big (and often prohibitive) expense to many small firms. If you are targeting a particular small firm, make sure you know whether or not they work with recruiters. Some firms won't even consider applicants who come through a headhunter. Consider the following scenario: a small firm is considering two similar applicants, one from a recruiter and the other who applies directly. The firm usually hires the person not represented by a recruiter because they won't have to pay tens of thousands of dollars in fees!

Ann Skalaski, founder and president of Skalaski Consulting, gives recent law grads the following sage advice: *"Regardless of whether you approach a recruiter for placement assistance or career advice, you will be best served if you can clearly communicate your abilities and goals."*

> **The bottom line:** You are more likely to find success using a recruiter if you are a candidate looking for a specialty position for which you have the requisite

background (i.e., seeking an IP position with an electrical engineering degree), or if you are trying to move to a region that you know nothing about. Otherwise, apply directly to the firm yourself. It takes more legwork, but you avoid the risk of your candidacy being adversely influenced by a search fee.

Commercial web sites

The Internet is the most obvious resource as you begin assembling your target list of small firm attorneys…but a little background will be helpful.

For example, did you know that both *Martindale.com* and *Lawyers.com* are populated by the same database of attorneys? It works like this: once a lawyer passes the bar, their contact information is posted on both sites, and the individuals are invited—for a fee—to expand their profile. If the attorney cannot be reached or declines to pay the fee, their names are entered but the accompanying information is limited to a physical address and no phone number or email. Another thing you should know is that *Martindale.com* is marketed more heavily to large firms and corporations, who use the site to find other large law firms and lawyers. Conversely, *Lawyers.com* is geared more towards the general public. This explains why doing the same type of search will result in a different number of hits. Going to *Martindale.com* in search of attorneys in, say, Yuma, Arizona, will result in 133 hits, while the same search at *Lawyers.com* will only yield 23 hits. Many attorneys know that *Martindale.com* is potentially more lucrative, so they will spend more of their advertising dollars on that site.

The scale and depth of a site's search function is another vital consideration when searching legal Web sites. Martindale.com offers a greater ability than Lawyers.com to narrow the search results. At Martindale, results can be narrowed by practice area, foreign languages, organization type, job title, and the attorney's admit state. A third site—Findlaw.com—also lets you search for small firm attorneys by geography and practice area. A fourth site—*West Legal Directory* (go to www.lawschool.westlaw.com)—is comprehensive and includes not only private firms but also city agencies and court listings, names of judges, and names of JAG attorneys. Some entries are perfunctory (name of the attorney, physical address, phone number), while others contain detailed profiles about the law firm, complete with a narrative on the firm's history and individual attorney biographies. You can also learn, for example, where an attorney attended law school, the size of his/her firm, the year of admission to the bar, and how much of the practice is devoted to particular practice areas broken down by percentage. Even more useful are entries that contain a list of documents that can be attributed to that attorney, including pleadings, motions and memoranda, trial court filings, jury instructions, cases, appellate briefs and even law journal articles. These documents are a gold mine of information when researching a particular attorney!

Law school directories

If your school is part of a consortium of law schools, its career services office probably has directories of private firms located in your area, and perhaps even in other cities and states. The information provided in these directories can include the size of the firm, the name of the hiring partner (where applicable), and the types of areas practiced.

Small firm web sites

A few words of caution: some small firms don't have an online presence, and some don't update their Web sites regularly. In addition, you shouldn't assume that the firm spends equal amount of time on all of the practice areas it lists on its site. It is more likely that the firm focuses on two or three areas, and only a small amount of time on the others. Example: Suppose ABC Firm states on its Web site that it focuses on"business transactions, health care law, commercial matters, and real estate."And suppose that as a former real estate agent, you are very interested in finding work in that area as a law clerk, so you send a resume and a targeted cover letter. It turns out that real estate only comprises about 10 percent of the firm's total practice, and that a single attorney works on those cases when the work does come in. The firm does practice real estate law; just not enough to support hiring another employee. *Information on a firm's Web site should be just a starting point in your research.* You will need to dig a little deeper in conversation with other attorneys, or colleagues who are former clerks or attorneys at the firm.

Bar associations

State and local bar associations have membership lists you can draw from, assuming they are willing to share that information. If they are not, look up the bar association's individual section lists, like the Environmental Law section or the Bankruptcy section. Often, the sections have executive councils listed on the Web site with the names and contact information for each section member. The ABA's General Practice, Solo and Small Firm Division has an extremely robust and active membership. The Division allows student memberships, it publishes a periodical dedicated to solo and small firm issues (*GP Solo Magazine*), and it has a wealth of information on what's going on nationally with solo and small firm attorneys. It also hosts a popular listserv (*Solosez*), which has more than 3,000 solo and small firm subscribers who actively discuss substantive topics. In addition, the constituencies of local and regional bar associations (like county bars) are almost always made up primarily of small firm lawyers. The same applies to organizations like the National Employment Lawyers Association and the National Lawyers Guild. They might also be more willing to share information about their attorney membership. And they are usually more willing to allow student membership or reduced rates for new attorneys.

Social media

More and more people are finding jobs with the help of social media. Whether it's Twitter, LinkedIn, Facebook, Google Plus, or the many other online networking sites, you should definitely include them in your small firm job search. And one of the best books on the topic is one by legal recruiter and former lawyer Amanda Ellis, author of *The 6Ps of the BIG 3 for Job-Seeking JDs: 60+ Ways to Get Hired Using Social Networking*. Another great resource is NALP's online series of guides on "e-professionalism" for law students and lawyers (www.nalp.org/eguides).

Legal media

You can often learn about the formation of a new small or mid-sized firm through a state bar's monthly magazine or a city's business journal. They are also occasionally covered by the National Law Journal and its affiliates. Take advantage of these announcements by offering yourself as a law clerk or attorney who can help with the firm's workload as they get acclimated to operating as a new firm. Here's an example of one such announcement in the National Law Journal, and how to capitalize on it:

> **Acquisition of Bond Firm Gives Polsinelli Shugart a Los Angeles Presence**
> Kansas City, Mo.-based Polsinelli Shughart has opened a Los Angeles office with the acquisition of Quateman LLP, California's largest woman-owned municipal bond law firm. Lisa Quateman, who founded her firm 22 years ago, is now managing partner of Polsinelli's Los Angeles office.

This sample article lists the name of the managing partner at the firm and its area of expertise. Students or attorneys interested in finance/business law should find out if there are any alumni working for the firm, and to send a resume offering their services as a law clerk or attorney. If there are no alumni, you might try and make contact directly to the managing partner. This should be done ASAP in order to get the jump on potential opportunities before they are snapped up. For example:

- In the case of a new or newly merged firm, you might simply send a note to the managing partner that says, *"Congratulations on the formation of your new firm"*…and then briefly introduce yourself.
- If you heard about the new firm from an existing contact, take the occasion to name-drop (*"Alice Bishop suggested I write because …"*).
- If you learned about the new firm from their Web site, send a note that *"this aspect of your firm appeals to me because …"*

In most cases, State Bar and local business journals also have a section that announces recent awards given to local attorneys and recent appointments to boards of directors and councils. For example: *Ari Smith, co-founder of Jones & Smith, a law firm that focuses on civil litigation issues, was selected to join the President's Advisory Council for McHenry County Community College…*or, *Sandy Flynn, an attorney for the law firm of Howard, Flynn & Moore was honored by the American Diabetes Association as top pro bono attorney for 2010.* Take the occasion to send a brief note of congratulations.

How to Start Looking

It is critically important that you communicate WHY you are reaching out to a particular attorney or contact. While the reason might seem obvious (e.g., you hope they give you a job), it's up to you to find a reason other than that so your communication seems less like a cold call. And it's just as important to remember that small firm attorneys are busy running a business, and that you can't assume that because you took time to send a cover letter and resume that it will be given the attention you think it deserves…especially if the attorney doesn't know you and your correspondence is unsolicited.

Name-dropping. Of all the potential "ins" available to you, old-fashioned name-dropping can be the most beneficial. But you must be discerning about using the name of the mutual contact. Having a five-minute conversation with someone at a social event does not necessarily mean it's acceptable to drop their name all over town. And if you do drop a name, make sure your contact consents (*"Alice Bishop suggested I write because …"*). It's a no-no to reference someone without letting them know you're doing it.

How else to get an "in" at a small firm?

You might learn from the attorney's Web site that both of you are active at a particular non-profit organization, or that you both attended the same law school or undergraduate institution. John Nasr, a law clerk at a midsized law firm in Phoenix, found his job that way:

"I emailed a bankruptcy partner at a local firm who earned a JD/MBA from the University of Oklahoma where I did my undergrad work. I met him for coffee one afternoon and followed-up about two months [later] to inquire about giving me the names of some local bankruptcy attorneys. He sent an email to six attorneys on my behalf, and I followed-up with each one individually. After having coffee with one of them about five weeks ago, [I learned] that her firm might be looking for an associate. They scheduled an interview about two weeks ago, and I got the offer."

Informational interviews. Informational interviews are an opportunity to learn more about the profession or a particular practice area…to build relationships within the profession…to practice your networking skills…to have a professional, articulate conversation…and to learn more about the person with whom you are speaking. What an informational interview is not is a job interview in disguise. And that's why informational interviews can be so rewarding, *because people are much more likely to talk about themselves and what they do when they do not feel like they are being pressured for a job.*

The first step in getting an informational interview is to reach out to the people in your network—by email or phone—and simply ask to take them out for a cup of coffee or to lunch. To improve your chances of acceptance, you might mention the name of a mutual acquaintance. Or refer to a blog post they wrote, or a case they worked on, or a law review article they wrote. And don't overlook non-attorneys among your contacts; your informational interview ought to be with anyone who might be able to provide useful information about the community you are trying to reach. Vic Massaglia, career counselor at University of Minnesota Law School, says, "[*Informational interviews*] *are meant to be less formal than a traditional interview, and the communication leading up to meeting should reflect this informality yet still be professional in tone.*" Massaglia says your message should include who you are (*"I'm a law student at …"*), how you found your contact (*"I'm not a stalker"*), and the reason for reaching out to your contact (*"to learn more about you and your work because I'm pursuing that area of the law"*).

It's that simple.

Once you've scheduled your informational interview, it's appropriate to send a thank you note that confirms your meeting. It might read something like this:

Hello Ms. Jones.

Thank you for agreeing to meet me for coffee at the May Street Deli at 8:15 a.m., on Friday, June 21st before your hearing. I look forward to learning about your career path, and hearing your perspective about practicing employment law.

Regards,
Bob

Robert Smith
University of Palm School of Law
Juris Doctor anticipated May, 2014
(904) 555-5555
rsmith@upslaw.edu

In preparation for the interview, develop some thoughtful, open-ended questions, and avoid canned questions that can be answered with a yes or a no. You will get a lot more useful information by tailoring your questions to the attorney's practice area, their firm, and their outside interests. Asking for an informational interview is a fairly simple process but it does require preparation. And the more focused you are, the more your contact will be able to help your job search move forward. A few additional suggestions:

- When requesting an informational interview, don't include a cover letter or a resume. The attorney might assume you're looking for a job in the guise of an informational interview.
- Allow about 20 minutes for the interview, and be flexible if the interview is going well and the attorney is willing to talk further.
- Most people will invite you to their office. If you happen to reach the attorney over the phone, have your questions ready if he or she wants to do the interview then and there.

The prep you do will help you generate questions for your interviewee. But if you get stuck, here are some examples:

What trends seem to be emerging from your practice area?
Tell me about your typical day at work?
What type of special education and/or training does your practice area require?
What do you enjoy/dislike about your work?

Are you active in any state or local bar associations? Any sections in particular?

Can you recommend anyone who could help me learn more about this practice area?

Attorneys are generally receptive and forthcoming if they're treated as a source of insight and information rather than a means to an end (a job). So, for 20 or 30 minutes, make like a sponge, and soak up all the information you can that bears on your job search. And while it's usually improper to ask for a job flat-out, 3Ls and new graduates can be more direct in terms of asking for part-time or project work. For example, you might say, "Feel free to pass my contact information along to anyone you know who might need help with a project." In this way, you become a resource if the attorney is ever contacted by a colleague who has some overflow work.

Send a thank you note within 24 hours. The giving of the attorney's time warrants a thank-you note, preferably hand-written on nice card stock, but an email will suffice. You should also mention a specific piece of information or fact from the interview that you found especially helpful. Be sure to note the details of your meeting in your notebook or spreadsheet, and stay in touch with the attorney.

One last thought: while you should never assume the meeting is actually a job interview in disguise, an informational interview is, in fact, just a heartbeat away from the real thing. So, be sure to act and dress accordingly, and arrive on time…and plan on doing most of the listening. In other words, treat the interviewee as you would any other potential employer because you never know whether down the road he or she could be your boss!

How to Market Yourself (and Stand Out)

In this economy, being a good student with practical experience is crucial to finding gainful employment. And yet many small-firm attorneys feel there is a little correlation between practice-readiness and high academic performance or law review experience. So, they tend to seek out law clerks and associates who can leverage prior experience (legal or non-legal), and can hit the ground running with little supervision.

Since skills and qualifications aren't always enough to get hired these days, you need to know your strengths and play to them whether you're in a job interview, or you're networking at a CLE event. To borrow an analogy from the business world, just making a product available won't get it flying off the shelves. Translation: if you don't know what's unique about your product—that is, you—it'll never sell. Marketing yourself might seem like an uncomfortable prospect, but—like it or not—it has become a critical component of the small firm job search. After all, you have worked incredibly hard for three years, and now have a valuable "product" to show for it, but no one will know about you unless you market yourself.

So, what are the best attributes of *your* "product"?

Your legal research & writing skills
Your ability to work well with others.
Your case-management ability
Your trial experience (as a student-attorney or as a practicing attorney)
Your work ethic
Your reputation as a fast learner

Does your *product* have any unique/special features?

Special knowledge and focus in a particular area of law
Professional experience prior to attending law school
Strong connections to the community
Special licensures (CPA, CFA, real estate license, teaching certification)
Ability to handle a case from beginning to end
Experience with client contact

If your grades are not your strong suit, emphasize the classes in which you did well and that would be important to the attorney you are targeting. For example, a family law attorney might not care so much that you tanked Constitutional Law, but will likely care very much that you did well in your Mediation Clinic. Another word on grades: regardless of your academic performance, you should highlight to the fullest extent possible your strong performance in legal research and writing classes. Across the board, you will find attorneys say that these skills are critical to the practice of law. If you can market yourself as a candidate who can write very well and perform efficient (cost-effective) legal research, it will go a long way towards putting you above other candidates.

But you must know about the product you are trying to sell. Assessing what it is about your skills and qualifications that make you a valuable commodity is a good place to start.

Don't ask for a job. Knowing what not to do when marketing yourself is a critical aspect of your job search because saying or doing the wrong thing can cause you to miss out on valuable opportunities. And what NOT to do is to ask directly for a job. This might seem counter-intuitive, but there are many reasons behind this:

- It might back your contacts into a corner by asking for something they're unable to give.
- It might have the effect of foreclosing any future conversations.
- Approaching your job search with "I need a job" tattooed on your forehead just might scare off more people than you think.

At some point, of course, you do have to let your contacts know that you are a job-seeker. But the point is to not make it the focal point of your conversation because the person with whom you're speaking may not be able to get you a job. However, you may learn something that helps get you a job, or your contact may know someone who is seeking help. So, instead of flat-out asking for a job, ask for information, ask for advice, or ask for additional resources (networking events, books, Web sites, or other contacts). This is a much better strategy considering that attorneys are almost always willing to give advice, for advice is plentiful and costs nothing to give. Second, many attorneys seek out opportunities to impart words of wisdom to law students and new lawyers who are seeking their advice. So soak up any and all information that can be used either directly or indirectly in your job search.

At some point in the conversation, it is almost guaranteed to come out that you are currently looking for work. And if you have made yourself out to be someone who is a good listener and who is genuinely interested in learning, it will be much more likely that the person you are speaking to will be willing to help you in your job search.

Stay current about small firm issues. One very easy way to get an "in" is to develop an ability to identify and discuss topical issues relevant to small firm attorneys. State bar committees are a great source of information. Start by getting involved with a section that interests you, and start reading the newsletters (including archived editions), blog posts and commentary.

The payoff might go something like this:

You meet a small firm attorney at a networking event, and the conversation turns toward his practice. You learn he is established in his field, and that his firm has grown in size over the last several years. The discussion leads to a bar journal article you read, and you mention how it might affect the attorney's firm. Whether or not the attorney has read the article, you have now added some value to the conversation, and potentially educated the attorney on an emerging trend of which he may not have been aware. Forwarding the attorney a copy of the article later is a really nice way to follow up.

Educating yourself can also provide you with opportunities to share helpful information. As a job-seeker you should always look for ways to create a "two-way street" with potential employers. In other words, don't just keep pushing yourself out to your contacts in hopes that they help you find a job. Look for ways to help them. An easy way is to subscribe to some RSS feeds that contain interesting articles that you can forward on to your contacts. Don't forget to include a brief description of the article in the body of the email along with a note that says: "I thought you might find this article interesting ..." Another way to build rapport is to watch for their name in the media (or set up a Google alert for their name or firm's name). Were they just honored as the local bar's Pro Bono Attorney of the Month, or just named to your state's Super Lawyers rankings for a particular practice area? Send a congratulatory note.

TWO PERSPECTIVES ON SMALL FIRM PRACTICE

In urban areas most small firms are largely oriented to litigation, usually representing individuals who have been injured or damaged in one way or another.

Many firms are specialized in labor matters, personal injury, medical malpractice, and other areas commonly affecting individuals. Income can vary widely. This size firm is also most common in smaller communities, whether a small town or neighborhood or suburb of a large city, and it represents a very different category of practice. You are more of a generalist, dealing with whatever comes in the door. This can be a risky practice because you cannot have expertise in the range of matters which come your way. The client wants quick and practical advice, and this is often all she or he can pay for. All lawyers, regardless of the size of firm in which they practice, have to face this issue professionally. In a small firm you simply face it more often, and there is a need for a sixth sense to know when to get more expert assistance. Importantly, do not be tempted to wing it to avoid the risk of losing a client when she or he considers dealing with a lawyer or firm with more expertise. At their best, these firms represent the most common vision people have of practicing lawyers representing real average people and businesses and personally solving or resolving their problems.

—Ralph G. Wrobley, Esq. Excerpt from Work, Life & the High Calling of the Law: A Managing Partner's Perspective (2010)

For some lawyers, untangling the tax code is challenging, stimulating, and generates a healthy revenue stream. Is it a good practice area for you? Not if you lack attention to detail or if tax law bores you to tears. Selecting the right practice area is an intensely personal decision, and what seems ideal on paper ... or works for others ... may not click for you. In fact, selecting the right practice for you is a lot like choosing a spouse or partner. First, there are such practical considerations as economic stability and general appeal, but —in law as in life—you can't thrive or find fulfillment without compatibility...and a healthy dose of passion.

Even if you have no prior work experience, you probably have a general sense of what types of matters you don't want to handle. In my own case, I started my practice with one specialization and wanted to expand. I also knew that family law, with all of its emotional baggage, or trusts and estates (which was incomprehensible to me in law school), weren't right for me. So I turned down cases in those areas from the beginning. By continuing to rule out areas that weren't a fit, I eventually settled on five main practice areas that worked for me (energy regulatory and renewables, court-appointed criminal work, appellate litigation, civil rights/employment law and small business litigation). Eventually, I phased out my court-appointed criminal work that no longer made sense from a financial perspective, and also small-business litigation because I didn't like state court practice. For some lawyers, choosing a practice area is an evolutionary process that involves a good bit of experimentation and trial and error. So if there are several areas of interest, feel free to sample a variety of different client matters. Also, offer to assist an experienced attorney in a particular practice area so you can learn what's involved without the pressure of handling an unfamiliar area on your own.

—CAROLYN ELEFANT, ESQ. EXCERPT FROM *SOLO BY CHOICE 2011/2012: HOW TO BE THE LAWYER YOU ALWAYS WANTED TO BE*

CHAPTER 7

How to Reach Out to Small Firms

If we were still in the 1980s, this section of the book wouldn't even exist. After all, back then there were only three ways a job-seeker could communicate with prospective employers: by phone (a land-line), by letter (aka snail mail), or in person. What a difference 30 years makes.

The latest communications technology—in the form of smartphones, tablets, and mobile job search apps—carries new protocols and new responsibilities for job-seekers. In short, the method you choose to initiate contact with small firm employers should not be taken lightly. For example, have you thought about whether your first contact should be over the phone or via email? Or, whether it's appropriate to send your resume and cover letter via fax? Or, why phone calls are a tricky, less-favored option…or what sort of message should you leave on voicemail…or whether it's appropriate to just show up at the attorney's office?

There are so many different ways to get in touch these days. It's important to have a plan of attack and a Plan B if your emails go unanswered, or if you continue to get an attorney's voicemail or office assistant.

Reaching out by email

Opinions differ on whether to use email as your first contact. Some say the impersonal nature of emails makes them easy to ignore, especially by a busy attorney who might get hundred of business emails each day not to mention the usual email spam. Still, there are some distinct advantages to initiating contact by email: a) it gives an attorney a chance to quickly scan your background, skills, and qualifications, b) you can carefully craft and edit your inquiry until it shines, and c) an email lets you attach a resume and/or cover letter so the attorney can make a quick assessment if you are someone they might be interested in hiring.

Q: Should you attach your resume as a separate file, or add it to the body of the email?

A: It depends on the purpose of your note. If you're applying for a job that you know exists, a more formal approach is warranted: send a separate cover letter with an attached resume. Include a brief note in the body of your cover message that indicates why you are writing and a list of the documents attached. If you are reaching out to request an informational interview, a less formal approach might be better received. In this case, attach your resume and include an abbreviated cover letter in the body of the email that identifies you, the name of the person who referred you, and what you are seeking. Note: do not use a cute email address. While lawstudentforhire@gmail.com might sound witty and ironic, you should keep it simple and straightforward; perhaps use the address assigned by your law school.

Reaching out by correspondence

As stated above, the danger of relying solely on emails is that it can get buried and ignored as "non-critical" by the recipient. So be ready to implement a Plan B, which is to send a paper resume and cover letter. You may not be aware, but many small firm attorneys say they pay greater attention to paper correspondence because they so rarely receive it! Paper might seem unfashionable, but—if what small firm attorneys say about snail mail is accurate—it might just get you noticed. Whether you initiate contact by email or mail, direct your letter to an actual person not just to the firm. Here are four options:

Option #1. Write to someone you know at the firm personally or through a contact (who agrees you can use their name).

Option #2. Direct your letter to an alumnus from your law school or from your undergraduate institution.

Option #3. Call the firm and ask who is in charge of hiring.

Option #4. Find the name of the most senior lawyer who seems to do the work you are interested in doing and direct your letter to that individual.

Reaching out by telephone

Phone calls—especially cold calls—are a less-favored method because of the intimidation factor. And yet some attorneys are impressed by candidates who have the courage to pick up a phone and articulate who they are and the purpose of their call. If you can do it, a phone pitch gives you an unrivaled opportunity to make a good first impression. It lets the listener hear your voice, and quickly assess how articulate you are, the extent to which you can listen and respond in kind, and the overall manner in which you conduct a conversation. These elements make phone contact superior to the two other, more passive forms—email and letters. If you do choose to initiate contact by phone, make it easy on yourself; draft a script that contains a 30-second "elevator pitch" (see Page 52) and practice (and practice some more) until you feel comfortable. In this way, you will sound poised, professional, and articulate instead of unsure, awkward, and nervous.

Contingency #1: What if your call goes to voicemail? Whatever you do, don't hang up without leaving a message. A brief message. No more than 20 seconds. After that, you have to assume the attorney will just skip over it. For this reason alone you should plan on practicing your elevator pitch over and over until it flows out smoothly.

Contingency #2: What if your call is directed to the attorney's office assistant? At all times and without fail, you should be extremely pleasant. Remember, the assistant is the gatekeeper to the attorney's time, and will not appreciate being spoken to rudely or in a manner that makes them think you have an absolute right to be immediately connected. And do not take it personally if you get the sense that you are being screened out…because you probably will be at first. Say who you are and why you are calling. If you are kind and pleasant to the assistant, it will be much more likely you will get connected to the attorney. It should be no surprise that messages from rude people often wind up getting "lost".

Reaching out with personal contact

If you have your heart set on working for a particular firm, consider stopping by unannounced. This might be considered a presumptuous move by a large firm, but at some smaller firms it is sometimes appreciated as initiative. In fact, it might just be the "x" factor that lands the job. Of course, you must show up as well-dressed as a lawyer appearing in court, and you should come with a resume, transcript, and writing sample…and ask to speak with the person in charge of hiring. Yes, it is an assertive approach, but many small firms appreciate that mentality!

Consider this true story: a law student we know stopped by a small bankruptcy law office with a resume in hand and asked if any of the attorneys needed help. One of them said, *"I don't have a need right now, but let me fax this [the resume] over to my wife who teaches law. Just last night she was complaining about how much work she has to do in researching her article."* The resume was faxed, the attorney's wife drove over to meet the student, and hired him on the spot. Not only that, but the student became the law professor's research assistant...and provided legal assistance at the attorney's firm whenever the workload warranted it.

DOING NOTHING IS NOT AN OPTION

By Richard L. Hermann, Esq.

Whenever an attorney job candidate I interviewed for my company presented a resume that did not address a lengthy time period between law school graduation and our interview, I posed this question: *"What have you been doing since you graduated from law school, other than studying for the bar examination?"* If the response was: *"Nothing. I've been looking for work full-time,"* I almost always concluded that the candidate would not be a desirable employee.

While job-hunting is often called a full-time job in itself, it really is not. You can both seek employment and do something else simultaneously without jeopardizing your job search. After all, lawyering is often much more than a full-time job. Just ask any major law firm associate about his or her "normal" 80+ hour weeks. If you are just job-hunting, period, you are sending a negative message to prospective employers. Employers want to see initiative. Moreover, doing something while job-hunting is a very effective way of overcoming a perceived experience gap. The array of possibilities open to you to gain experience are vast.

Here are some of the things that my legal career counseling clients who were fresh out of law school and jobless for an extended period of time did to "fill-in-the-blanks."

ADR Certification and Opportunities

Getting certified as an Alternative Dispute Resolution (ADR) professional can be done easily, quickly and relatively cheaply. Most ADR certification programs take only approximately one week. Getting certified as a mediator is the first step toward gaining experience doing actual mediations. Certification programs are abundant, and there is a lot of good information about them online. If you have a choice between an onsite or online program, choose the former. Mediation is a very people-intensive, face-to-face undertaking, and you are likely to see that mirrored in the role-playing that is central to most ADR training programs. If an onsite program is impossible, then online ADR training is acceptable. Once you have obtained your ADR certification, there are a large and growing number of organizations for which you can volunteer in order to gain experience. Chief among these are state and local courts. The National Center for State Courts (www.ncsc.org) has identified more than 1,300 court-connected ADR programs at state and local levels throughout the country. They consist of programs for small claims, probate, juvenile, family, criminal, civil and appellate matters. In most jurisdictions, cases are referred to ADR by judges, and most mediators are volunteers.

Assigned Counsel

An assigned counsel is an attorney appointed by a court to represent an indigent person. Unlike ADR referral programs, which almost always rely on volunteer attorneys, assigned counsel appointments are paid assignments. In New York State, for example, assigned counsel is paid $75/hour for Family Court cases and felonies, and $60/hour for misdemeanors and lesser charges. This is an excellent way to both gain some experience and fill in a gap in your resume. State indigent defense systems are all over the map when it comes to organization and funding. In New York, for example, the system is a county one, with no state administration. In contrast, neighboring New Jersey has a statewide public defender system with trial and appellate attorneys throughout the state. However, when caseloads expand beyond the New Jersey Public Defender's ability to handle them, private attorneys are hired on a contract basis to deal with the overage. For more information about this opportunity, see www.nacdl.org.

Volunteering

The Great Recession has put a severe crimp on legal services and legal aid programs that rely for their funding on a combination of government appropriations, grants, and private contributions. Legal assistance programs are always under severe budgetary strain, even in good economic times. Consequently, they always need volunteer attorneys to help them cope with their caseloads. Moreover, in times of economic crisis, their caseloads increase as more and more families and individuals fall below the poverty line. The federal Legal Services Corporation (www.lsc.gov) funds 136 independent nonprofit legal aid programs with more than 900 offices that provide legal assistance to low-income individuals and families throughout the country. In addition, many states also maintain and fund civil legal aid programs for their residents. These are often funded by a combination of state appropriations and the interest earned by attorney trust accounts. Overall, there are several thousand legal aid programs that have volunteer opportunities for attorneys available.

Contract Lawyering

This has become a fall-back of last resort for unemployed lawyers. And given the high number of experienced attorneys who lost, and continue to lose, their jobs during the Great Recession, contract lawyering is not quite the safety net that it used to be. It has actually become somewhat competitive in certain cities, such as New York, San Francisco, Los Angeles, Miami and Washington, DC. Nevertheless, it is still a possibility if nothing else pans out. The biggest problem with contract lawyering, aside from the numbing nature of much of the work (and the low pay), is that it is likely to be more time-consuming than any of the other options discussed in this chapter. And you will still need some time (and energy) to hunt for a job.

Do not give prospective employers a reason to reject you because they think that you are lazy or unmotivated. Demonstrating initiative and the need to keep your legal skills fresh can count for a lot with employers.

RICHARD L. HERMANN, ESQ.
EXCERPT, *THE NEW LAWYER'S SURVIVAL GUIDE, VOL. 1: FROM LEMONS TO LEMONADE IN THE NEW LEGAL JOB MARKET* (2012)

CHAPTER 8

Networking: Planned Events & Chance Encounters

When it comes to a small firm job search, we can't overemphasize the importance of networking. Especially when an estimated 75 percent of all legal positions obtained outside of OCI programs are obtained as a result of networking. And by all accounts, 70 to 80 percent of the positions filled with small firms are filled by word-of-mouth (i.e., networking), which means you won't ever see those positions advertised. Still not convinced?

Spend a few moments studying the chart below, and see how many thousands of law graduates found jobs with small and midsized firms through networking and referrals.

JOB SOURCE BY EMPLOYER TYPE FOR CLASS OF 2010

(Percent of positions obtained from each source for size law firm)

Law Firms (15,057)	Fall OCI	Pre-law Employer	Job Fair	Self-initiated	Job Listing	Referral	Started Own Practice	Other*
# Lawyers								
2–10 (5,654)	1.2	6.1	0.3	31.4	19.6	25.5	2.8	13.1
11–25 (1,337)	12.1	5.5	1.0	25.6	19.0	24.5	0.0	12.3
26–50 (829)	25.1	5.0	1.1	23.5	15.8	18.9	0.0	10.6
51–100 (679)	35.6	4.3	2.2	19.2	11.0	14.4	0.0	13.3
101+ (5,066)	68.2	2.6	6.4	9.3	3.2	5.6	0.0	4.8

* Includes Spring OCI, temp agencies, commercial Internet sites, and other means.

Excerpt from NALP's JOBS & JDS:EMPLOYMENT AND SALARIES FOR NEW LAW GRADUATES (2011).

Why Networking is a Big Deal

Networking is about making connections and building professional relationships for short- and long-term mutual benefit. It's that simple.

We appreciate that for many law students, new grads (and even experienced lawyers), the mere mention of networking has a visceral impact (i.e., anxiety, sweating), and generates strong avoidance reaction (as in, *I'd rather have a tooth extracted*). These are common reactions, but they must not get in the way of your making use of this incredibly…powerful…technique. Networking is a big deal. After all, you might look great on paper, but resumes and cover letters will only get you so far. People hire people not just a set of skills and qualifications. Small firm employers also want a pleasant personality, clear and articulate speech, and a professional demeanor; qualities that don't come across on paper, but can emerge in an informal, 10-minute face-to-face encounter. You want another argument for networking? Take another look at the chart above: statistically speaking, networking was responsible for getting thousands of Class of 2010 lawyers into small firms…and, that same networking ability will later help them bring new business into their firm.

Networking is a process with three critical components: a) developing your list of contacts, b) meeting with those contacts, and c) following up.

And that advice is worth repeating …

Develop a list of contacts
Meet with your list of contacts
Follow up with your list of contacts

Leaving out even one of these components and you will sabotage all your hard work.

Developing a List of Contacts

Establishing your contacts is the first step. Don't limit your list just to those who have some connection to the legal community. Your Aunt Jane, for example, might have attended high school with the current partner of a law firm in town, and it just so happens they still keep in touch. The point is… you don't need to be pals with the rich and famous, or the managing partner of the largest firm in town, to build an effective network. Your contacts might come through hobbies, sports, clubs, or religious or community groups. Go through your address book and cell phone memory. Many new attorneys eventually get hired on the recommendation of a personal contact: dentist, doctor, teammate, teammate's father, roommate, roommate's sister, study group, even a second cousin-once-removed. Start with who you know. The idea is a) to create a target network of people who work in your target area, and b) to create a network that can lead you to those who work in that area.

Prepare an elevator pitch. An elevator pitch is a short, detailed, 15-30-second description of who you are, what you hope to accomplish with your job search, and something about your strengths, skills, and experiences. Spoken with energy and enthusiasm, your pitch promotes you in a way that is succinct and not overly boastful, and it allows the listener to ask follow-up questions and actually remember you later. Once you have the content of your pitch in place, practice it with a spouse, friend, family member…or in front of the mirror. Get comfortable with it. If you get stuck creating your pitch, go to www.15secondpitch.com or www.elevatorspeech. com.

In the meantime, here are a few examples:

"Hi, my name is Courtney Grimes. I'm a second-year law student at XYZ School of Law and I'm interested in personal injury law. Trial practice has always been fascinating to me and I did very well in my trial advocacy class last semester. I'm really interested in meeting the speaker and hearing what she has to say about recent developments on the topic of limitations on damage awards."

"Hi, my name is Fred Satchel, and I'm a third-year law student at ABC School of Law. Environmental law has always been intriguing to me having grown up in the Pacific Northwest, but I'm still exploring as I'm not sure if it's an area I want to commit to fully."

"Hi, my name is Susan Bowen. I'm originally from Boston where I was a ballet instructor, but I discovered my true passion for the law which brought me to ABC Law School in Texas, where I'm enjoying learning about entertainment and business law."

Meeting Your List of Contacts

Networking events generally fall into two categories.

Planned events include law school lunches, award ceremonies, CLEs, and events featuring a speaker. In these situations, prepare for the networking portion of the event by learning as much as you can about the attendees and the speaker as an icebreaker to open conversations. When you arrive, mingle. Just showing up is a good start…but not enough, especially if you remain in the corner, or worse, retreat to a table with other nervous law students.

The second networking category is the *chance encounter,* which is also rich with possibilities. Chance encounters might include bar association socials or alumni receptions…or sitting beside someone at a lunch or on a red-eye flight to Chicago…or just striking up a conversation with someone in line at the bank. All of the above are occasions for your elevator pitch (you know, the one you've been practicing).

Planned or unplanned, most of us are reluctant to network because of a fear of failure, rejection, or because it feels awkward to promote ourselves. *The secret to really good networking, though—that is, networking that works—is to attend events with the goal of helping at least one person.* By this approach, you essentially create a bond between yourself and the attorney(s) you meet. You might steer them to the person in charge of choosing adjunct faculty, or connect them to the Moot Court Executive Board because they want to act as a judge. The opportunities to help are limitless, so keep eyes and ears open.

Here are some other tips:

Don't be late. This might seem obvious, but often an event will have about 30 minutes built into the beginning to allow for networking. You don't want to miss it!

The handshake. Practice your handshake. Seriously. The traditional handshake calls for a firm grip and direct eye contact. Shaking hands is gender neutral; all handshakes are treated equally. Remember, you only get one chance to make a first impression.

Put JOB out of your mind. Don't walk into a networking event or meeting thinking you have to secure an offer before the event is over or you failed miserably. That approach will make you kind of scary, so relax.

Prepare some starter questions. What tends to be an obstacle is a perception that you must have some sort of a snappy comeback, or bring some brilliant insight into a networking conversation. The only thing you need to bring to the table are a few simple conversation openers…and then listen. For example, *What brings you to this particular event? What practice areas do you focus on? How is the economy affecting your business?*

Listen and maintain eye contact. Did you ever notice that the most successful networkers make you feel like you're the most important person in the room at that moment? It works for them; it can work for you. When you're engaged in a networking conversation, maintain eye contact and show interest. Nod your head and interject a "mm-hmm" every now and again. Better yet, ask a question based on something the attorney says. Networking conversations should be kept to around five minutes, so be considerate of the other person's time. When you are ready to leave one conversation and move to another, let the other person know how pleased you were to have met them and move on. Note: while you're engaged in one conversation, don't scan the room looking for your buddy or the panelist you just heard speak. And never, NEVER check your cell phone for texts or even take a call (in fact, mute your phone before walking into the room).

It's not about you. It's a fact of life: most people love talking about themselves. You will be surprised at how easy it is to get attorneys to get talking about…*what types of careers they embarked on prior to their current position, how they got their current position, their advice on breaking into the field, what networking events they themselves attend, and what a typical day looks like in their practice.* The best networking questions prompt the other person to talk about his or her work, employer, family, or personal interests. If you don't know anyone at the event, start up a conversation with someone who is standing by him or herself. You will be helping them, and it will restore your confidence.

Stay flexible. Let's say you're interested in practicing family law, but you run into a securities litigation attorney at the networking event. Most students might assume that attorney couldn't possibly help them in their job search, and they might make only a half-hearted attempt at conversation. Big mistake. Chances are that attorney knows a great family law lawyer who works down the hall, and he or she keeps in touch with colleagues from her graduating class, and knows who has a family law practice and who could use some help.

Don't miss the big picture: Some job seekers tune out if they hear an attorney say, *"I'd love to help you, but we're just not hiring right now."* If you tune out—or worse, bring the conversation to an abrupt conclusion—you make it seem it as if you were just using the occasion as a means to get a job. If so, you missed the big picture: the chance to learn from the attorney. Try this approach: *"It's understandable that your firm isn't hiring right now, with the state of the economy being what it is. But if you happen to know of anyone who is currently looking for part-time help, or even help with a project, please feel free to pass my name along."*

Bring a buddy or a teammate. Bring someone who is interested in a different practice area. That way, you avoid competition, and it allows you to meet up at the end of the event and compare notes. But don't use your friend as a crutch. If the two of you wind up talking to no one but each other, the only thing you have accomplished is that you would have both missed out on potential opportunities.

Bring business cards. Whether it's a planned event or a chance encounter, don't leave home without business cards. But offer them only to those with whom you are genuinely interested in following up. If you hand one to a small firm attorney, don't hold your breath waiting for them to follow up. Small firms expect you to contact them!

What about the cards you receive? Jot a few notes on the back to remind you of your meeting, and add an interesting fact about the conversation for your follow-up. Store the cards so you can use them later. Final note: when it comes to business cards, don't make the mistake of one overzealous law student. When handed an attorney's card at a reception, the student pulled out his cell phone and snapped a picture of the attorney with the card held next to his face so he could "remember him" better! When last seen, the shocked attorney was scanning the room for security.

The Follow-Up

> *"Don't just send out a resume and hope for a call-back. Pound the pavement. Law firm partners are busy, so follow up even if you have to go visit them at their office. They know they need help, but you need to make sure you are there when they decide to hire someone."*—JOSEPH (CLASS OF 2007)

The whole point of networking is to develop fruitful relationships. We recommended you follow up with an email within 48 hours of making initial contact.

Many a job-seeker works hard to find meaningful contacts and initiate conversations, and then…they don't follow up. *Failing to follow up is one of the most common mistakes that job-seekers make.* Why? Because following up takes time, and it requires discipline to keep a record of those you contacted, what you discussed, and how the original connection was made. Naturally, it's frustrating when you don't see immediate results. And if there is no response to your email, you're inclined to assume your contact didn't want to talk to you in the first place, and to just forget the conversation never happened.

Don't give up; there's too much at stake.

If you don't hear anything right away, follow up again in two or three months. This time update your contact with a pleasant note about how your semester is going...or send them an interesting article...or alert them to a seminar at the law school...or invite them to participate on a panel or act as a moot court judge...or ask to shadow them for a day or attend their trial or observe their deposition...or make yourself available for project work. Your networking contact will appreciate your proactive outreach especially if you provide them with helpful information. Remember, potential employers need to be reminded, and it's YOUR job to get them to remember you.

Author Ari Kaplan (*Reinventing Professional Services: Building Your Business in the Digital Marketplace*) cautions against impatience:

> *"As professionals and professional school students, we tend to be impatient and are often easily dissuaded. If you call someone once and don't hear back, do you simply give up? What is your practice for reconnecting with someone; a LinkedIn invitation and you're done?"*

What stymies most job-seekers is not knowing what to say in a follow-up. Just remember this: the main idea is to have some substance to your follow-up other than the fact that you are looking for a job. And your follow-up should be sincere, and express a desire to continue the rapport that was established at the original meeting. Then, and only then, can you communicate the fact that you are hoping to get something out of your relationship.

Here's an example:

> Dear Wayne,
>
> I hope all is well since we last spoke at the county bar mixer last month. Did your daughter's basketball team make it to the finals this season?
>
> Since we met, I've taken your advice and joined the bar's corporate counsel section. In fact, I've already made a couple of great connections there. Thank you for that very helpful suggestion.
>
> I'm still working toward finding summer employment. So, if you happen to know of any colleagues looking to hire, feel free to forward my resume.
>
> I hope to see you again in the near future.
>
> Best,
> Sam Student

This example illustrates one effective reason to follow up: to thank the contact for a helpful piece of advice. This is an especially powerful because Wayne now feels good about having done something to help Sam in his career. As a consequence, Wayne will very likely remember Sam by virtue of his outreach. Here are some other reasons you can employ to make your follow-up more meaningful:

- Update your contact on how the semester is going (especially after graduation!)
- Send them an interesting article
- Let your contact know about an interesting seminar at the law school (or outside of school)
- Provide updates on the school (usually only relevant for alumni)
- Extend an invitation to participate on a panel or act as a moot court judge
- Ask to "shadow" your contact at trial or to observe a deposition
- Make yourself available for project work

What NOT to say

Your follow-up should not be used in a way that makes the person feel like he is a means to an end. For example:

> Dear Wayne,
> You might remember meeting me at last month's county bar function. Have your hiring needs changed since we last met?
>
> Sincerely,
> Sam Student

As we've said before, networking requires discipline. For every contact in your database, you should know how you met that person, where the meeting occurred, who referred you, and the date(s) you followed up. Failing to keep good records can cause you to make a mistake in your facts, and worse, to overlook some great opportunities. Keep track with a notebook, a spreadsheet, a database tracking software, or one of the many contact management programs (Google has a free one). According to Eric Robinson, a 2010 graduate of Arizona State University's Sandra Day O'Connor College of Law, "It's important to be persistent. I could have said no to being on a local triathlon committee, and to everything I was asked to participate in that wasn't directly related to law school or finding a job. But I kept at it and maintaining my relationships by sending an email every couple of months, and to have lunch roughly every month."

Your Post-Networking Strategy

As you know, bar associations are usually grouped by practice areas or "sections". These sections offer a wealth of opportunity for small firm job seekers.

Call to get the name of the chairperson of the small firm section, or the section for which you have the most interest. Then call the chairperson and introduce yourself. Most lawyers, despite their work load, will welcome a call from a recent law school graduate interested in making his or her mark. Introduce yourself and briefly explain your interest in working at a small firm or in a particular field. Most sections meet monthly. Find out when the next meeting is scheduled, and make a point to be there. The chairperson may introduce you to other members. If not, take it upon yourself to circulate and meet prospective employers and ask for their business cards. See Appendix B for the list of small firm sections.

Other resources:

- Bar associations have membership directories. In some areas, they're referred to as "The Legal," (as in "Your old address is still in the Legal"). It's a wealth of information about the practice of law in your area. In addition to an alphabetical listing of attorneys, The Legal contains areas of specialties and advertisements.
- Your county law reporter has a classified ads section, and legal employers typically advertise there instead of a newspaper of general circulation.
- The small firm or solo bar sections of the bar sponsor periodic CLEs. If you're still in law school, you might be eligible for a discount or even a fee waiver in exchange for helping with registration. If you attend, you'll find yourself in a roomful of small firm practitioners. Ask their opinions and experiences, and tell them what you are seeking. Talk to the speakers after their presentations. Get their business cards and follow up with an email or letter.
- Project work can go a long way towards developing your network. If you can give yourself time to complete, say, three or four projects for different small firm attorneys during the course of a semester, that means at least four more attorneys will know about you and your work product.

Volunteering

Whether you offer to help with a food drive, or collect and distribute toys for tots, or work elbow-to-elbow with other attorneys on a Habitat for Humanity project, your volunteering opens the possibility of networking with other attorneys. Not only are you helping others and adding a few lines to your resume, you would be making real-time contact with attorneys in a casual setting. Interested in practicing family law? Try volunteering as a *guardian at litem* to help a child in need. In doing so, you gain first-hand experience on the inner workings of the system while you become familiar with the interaction between the court, state agencies and private bar.

Here are some examples from actual job-seekers:

"At a lunch sponsored by my law school, I was introduced to an attorney who had served in the Marines in the Vietnam War. When he learned I had come to law school after serving as a Navy pilot, we chatted about military experiences. At the end of the lunch, he offered to help me get on the Board of Directors of a nonprofit organization that helps homeless veterans. Within a year, I made more than two dozen significant professional contacts within the legal community."

"I recently went to lunch with an attorney, and we discovered a common interest in triathlon competitions. When he asked if I would be willing to help start a triathlon in our area, I said yes. Next thing I know, I'm on the formation committee, some of whose members were lawyers. We met for six or seven months, and I got to ask them about job searching and life at a small firm. [Then, out of the blue], one of the committee's attorneys asked if I was ready to start work at his small firm. Of course I said yes. Because of that one [networking lunch], I was able to turn it into a job."

Networking is a capital investment, and one that take time to yield a tangible benefit. The more time you invest, the more likely it is you will set events in motion that will lead to a job. All it takes is for one attorney you meet to forward your resume along to all of their contacts, and you wind up with an offer. But that serendipitous process can't unfold unless you put it into motion.

CHAPTER 9

Resumes & Cover Letters for the Small Firm

As a job seeker, you've probably read more books on resumes and cover letters than you care to remember. And you've probably already exhausted the efforts of your school's career services office. So, in this chapter we promise not to rehash the obvious mechanics of resume and cover letter writing, and instead focus on the special considerations that apply just to the small firm job market.

For example, did you know …

- You should list high grades only in areas practiced by the firm to which you are applying. Family law firms for example won't care much that you got an "A" in Constitutional Law; in fact, it could be distracting.
- You should include a "community service section" in your resume that details dates and descriptions of your activities. Experiences that demonstrate your commitment to the public interest can go a long way toward showing a small firm that you are in it for the long haul, and that you recognize the value in community involvement.
- You should include an "interests" section in your resume. Your outside interests are a great way to create a rapport with a small firm.
- You should highlight "core competencies" that apply to the job for which you're applying (see chapters 16-20). For example, if one of your core skills is technological, makes sure your resume reflects that; it makes you a more marketable candidate.
- But you should not skimp on describing your work experience! For some reason, many job seekers become strangely mute when it comes to describing their previous experiences. Big mistake; don't skimp. Small firms need to know exactly what you did, for whom, and for how long, as an assessment of whether or not you are qualified for the position.

Consider the advice of Tyler Carroll, a 2010 law graduate from Arizona State University:

"Small firms get a lot of resumes, not just from law students but from experienced attorneys. So, it's important that your resume focus on what makes you unique. [In my case] my jobs were recognizable; externships, research assistant positions, etc. But it's also important for employers to get a clear picture of what you did on those jobs so that if they say, 'I need someone to research an insurance issue,' and one of the candidates worked for an insurance attorney, they know she'll do a good job. Another example is a firm that looks at a resume and says, 'This person was a Westlaw representative, and since Westlaw is our primary research vehicle I know he'll do a good job.' [Making sure employers get a clear picture of what you did] can help them make the mental connections they need to give you the job"

But there's more to a resume than meets the eye.

For new law grads especially, resumes can serve a second, less obvious function in the competitive small firm job market. Used smartly, your resume can be used as an educational tool that might earn you a second look from the employer. Here's how it works: when you follow up the mailing of your resume (you were going to do that anyway, right?), you let the employer know you sent the resume so he or she could *get to know you better.* That phrase is important. It puts the attorney on notice that you have no expectation of a job, but merely wish to alert them to your unique qualifications (and availability, of course). This notion of a resume-as-educational tool takes a lot of pressure off the employer, and makes it more likely that he or she will want to read it and help. In fact, once they read your resume, the hiring attorney might be pleasantly surprised to learn that you both attended the same law school or undergraduate institution, or that you both volunteer for the same non-profit group, or that you both share a passion for rock climbing, or swing dancing, or French cuisine.

> Never underestimate the power of a shared affinity.

The following example, based on one student's experience, illustrates the power of the resume-as-educational tool:

A student we know met a criminal defense attorney at a networking function, and struck up a brief conversation because of his interest in criminal defense. Soon afterward, the student emailed the attorney, and thanked him for educating him on the practice of criminal defense. Attached to the email was a resume, and the student invited the attorney to forward it to any of his colleagues who could use some help. As the attorney read the resume, he learned that the student had worked fulltime through college, was bilingual, and was a native to that particular state. Seeing that the student had a strong work ethic, knew the area, and could help him translate with his Spanish-speaking clients, he offered him a project. A job!

The story could easily have taken a different direction: the defense attorney might not have had any immediate need for help, but knew of a colleague with a big new project who needed a law student's help. If it hadn't been for the student sending the resume (and, of course, attending the network function in the first place), the student would have never come to the attention of the second lawyer.

Looking for Work Out-of-State

Are you considering moving to a new city?

Did you know that moving to a new area away from home, or away from where you attended law school, can put you at a disadvantage over new lawyers who have spent several years (or perhaps their whole lives) cultivating local relationships? It might seem exciting to leave the East Coast for, say, San Francisco or Seattle, but it's not very realistic to just pack up and move in the hope that "it all works out." That doesn't mean that many graduates have not struck out to a new location—urban or rural—and found success. The key is to have a realistic plan. Here are some questions to consider:

Do you thrive in metropolitan areas, or would you prefer a more rural setting?
Do you want to stay near the law school after graduation, or will you return to
*   your home town?*
Do you have young children whose education will be factor?
What are your financial needs?

If you're really determined to work out-of-state, use every means at your disposal online and offline to research your target area. That means spending as much time there as you can—weekends, winter break, spring break—before graduation. Read local/regional publications to learn who the key players are in a particular practice area, and set up informational interviews beforehand (see Chapter 6). When sitting down with your contacts, be prepared to get specific about why you want to work in that community. Law firms are generally skeptical of candidates who do not already have ties to the community for fear they will pack up and leave soon after relocating. When asked what factors she believed lead to an offer, one young attorney said: *"They were mainly interested in the fact that I intended to live in the Savannah (Georgia) area for a long time. They wanted someone who would remain here permanently."*

Note: don't forget to ask for "reciprocity" while you are visiting!

Reciprocity, of course, is the policy that allows law schools to provide reasonable access to their career resources for students and graduates from other law schools that agree to provide similar services. Policies vary from school to school, so be sure to first look at each school's policy (usually posted on its Web site). Many schools block reciprocity during OCI months, and others only allow one visit per geographic area (which means you will only get it at one school in Chicago). One more thing: don't let a region's climate dictate your preferences. The Southwest may feel like an oven in summer, but the heat might eliminate some of the competition in the job market.

COVER LETTERS: DO YOUR DUE DILIGENCE

Dwane Cates, founder and managing partner of a small law firm in Phoenix, says he discards two or three resumes a week simply because the job-seekers failed in their due diligence. *"They might say they are interested in construction law,"* says Cates, *"But they don't bother to find out that we are a criminal defense firm."* Cover letters for small law firms are not much different from any legal cover letter—that is, they are brief, polished, and free of spelling and grammatical errors—BUT they also observe these additional conventions:

Targeting. You must research the firm and target your materials to the particular firm. Small firm employers can smell a generic cover letter a mile away.

Length. You should think quality not quantity. It's unnecessary to draft a lengthy cover letter that explains everything about you. Focus on what the firm wants to hear, and highlight only those elements in your resume that matter to the firm.

Geography. You should know that small law firms prefer their attorneys who live in the area and have local connections (schools, associations, religious organizations) in the hopes of bringing in new business.

The Unsolicited (Cold) Resume
Do unsolicited resumes get results?

No, they don't, says managing partner Dwane Cates. *"I don't pay much attention to unsolicited resumes that land on my desk, mainly because I know that it takes little or no effort to drop one in the mail."*

Yes, they do, says law firm partner Mike Holden. *"Two of my last four hires were [from] letters that hit my desk unsolicited at the right time, with no advertisement for a position. We had recently lost an associate and had a big case come in, and* *one of the resumes intrigued me. It was [solid], the [student] had done well in law school, and provided a strong writing sample. And [he] got a job out of it."*

Whether or not you choose to send unsolicited resumes, the cover letter must be personalized and not generic. Use your "in" to get the reader's attention (see Chapter 6, *How to Start Looking*). Think about it in this way: if you were a small firm attorney working a 12-hour day and not actively seeking to hire, would you bother looking at an unsolicited resume? You must give the attorney one or more good reasons to stop what he or she is doing, and pay attention to you as a candidate. When you do come across a job posting for a small firm, you can expect the description to be fairly specific as to the skills and qualifications sought. That specificity should make it easier to draft a *personalized* not generic response.

Here is a sample small firm job posting:

"Opportunity for a second-year law student to learn estate planning/probate/trust administration/guardian and conservatorships in a small firm setting. Duties vary from drafting pleadings to clerical work. Candidate should be mature, dependable, and have an ability to interact with elderly clients. Flexible hours within a normal workday/week. No nights or weekends."

And the response:

March 13, 2012

Mr. Paul Stevens
5814 W. Sesame Lane, Suite 300
Mesa AZ 85252

Dear Mr. Stevens:

I was pleased to see your advertisement listed on my law school's job bank because I feel my background and interests are well-suited for this particular position.

I am just wrapping up a summer externship at the Superior Court with Commissioner Jones in the Probate Division, and I am eager to continue learning about probate law. I entered my summer externship having almost no idea what probate law was. Now, after two months, I have a strong grasp of the fundamental concepts, and I am looking forward to building upon the knowledge I acquired this summer.

As a law student, I am excited about the possibility of learning the broad range of issues and experiences that probate law offers, and I am ready to learn about the various skills and responsibilities needed to succeed in this area of law.

Thank you for taking the time to review my qualifications. I look forward to talking to you.

Sincerely,
Tyler Oats

THE LEGAL JOB HUNTER'S 11 BIGGEST MISTAKES
By Richard L. Hermann, Esq.

Mistake #1. Failing to Identify Likely Employers. Sending mass-mailed applications to hundreds of employers simply because they are there and happen to hire attorneys from time-to-time is a complete waste of time, money and energy. Targeting employers is the name of the game, played correctly. Submitting job applications to just 10 employers who you have thoroughly researched and who you have concluded are compatible with your career goals, values and expectations, will almost always reap greater rewards than mass mailing/emailing applications to 1,000 employers extracted from Martindale Hubbell or "identified" by a resume mailing service.

Mistake #2. Not Searching ALL the Legal Job Ads. Not every legal job ad online or in the newspapers contains the words "attorney, law or legal." Whenever I ask lawyers what search terms they use, these are the Big Three. The growth in JD-preferred positions and other law-related positions means that you are doing yourself a serious disservice if you don't expand your searches to include search terms such as "compliance," "enforcement," "licensing," "contract," "regulatory" and many others.

Mistake #3. Writing Only One Resume. I have yet to meet a law student or attorney, entry-level or experienced, who could conduct a thorough job search relying on only a single, "one-size-fits-all" resume. Different employers require targeted applications. Using the same resume for every job opportunity diminishes your chances of being invited to an interview.

Mistake #4. Cramming Everything On a Single Page. Resumes that are overflowing with type, lack acceptable margins, or employ tiny type fonts that are difficult to read send a negative message to an employer. They are intimidating, to say the least, and few employers look forward to slogging their way through such type-rich documents with enthusiasm.

Mistake #5. Failing to Proofread Your Application Documents. I find grammatical mistakes—typographical errors, misspellings, the wrong tense, the absence of parallel construction, etc.—in more than 50 percent of the attorney application documents I see. When I hired attorneys, an error of this kind meant automatic rejection, regardless of how impressive the candidate was otherwise. My concern was always that, if this person was going to represent my company in writing, then errors such as this were unacceptable. Most legal employers have the same attitude. The careless need not apply.

Mistake #6. Revealing Too Much About Yourself. Under most circumstances, you need to be very careful if your application materials reveal a political preference, religious affiliation, or some other feature of your life that might be viewed askance by a prospective employer. A highly accomplished client of mine was general counsel to a prominent business that was a wholly-owned subsidiary of a very controversial, non-mainstream church. Over time, my client suspected that he was being summarily rejected for every position to which he applied because of bias against the church. Once he omitted mention of the church and just listed the business, interviews began coming his way.

Mistake #7. Relying on Letters of Recommendation. Increasingly, I run across law students and entry-level attorneys who claim that they cannot come up with any references, but have several letters of recommendation that they intend to submit to prospective employers as a substitute. Letters of recommendation are a poor substitute. Employers want to talk, person-to-person, to your references. They tend to discount letters of recommendation because they generally all read the same, full of excessive praise and laudatory language. Worse, those that do not contain such immoderate language about you are perceived even more negatively. The only time you should rely on a letter of recommendation is if you simply cannot find anyone to serve as a professional reference.

Mistake #8. Including Personal References. The only time to proffer a personal reference is if it is specifically requested by the employer. This rarely happens. Employers want to see professional references—current or former employers, professors, opposing counsel in cases you might have argued as a special 3L admittee under the state bar rules in the state where you attended law school, judges or hearing officers before whom you have appeared.

Mistake #9. Sending Unrequested Materials with Your Resume. Employers dislike being inundated with paper (or its electronic equivalent). If they ask for a resume and cover letter, send them a resume and cover letter, period.

Mistake #10. Not Making Sure Your Application Gets There. One of the most stunning job search oversights in my opinion is the failure of legal job candidates to follow-up on their applications. The road to job search success is littered with the detritus of applications that never made it to the employer. While this was a fairly minor issue in the pre-Internet era when reliance on the U.S. Postal Service or an overnight service was quite reliable, it is a much bigger issue now, when applications often can and do get lost in the "ether." Call or email the employer to confirm that your application arrived.

Mistake #11. Relocating Without Research. Often, legal job hunters assume that a geographic move is going to solve their career problems. It may, but before you pick up and move, do your due diligence regarding the new location and its legal opportunities. There is an immense amount of online information with which to compare geographic areas with respect to the number of attorneys per capita, cost of living, quality of life, client demographics, industries and much more.

By Richard L. Hermann, Esq.

Excerpt, *The New Lawyer's Survival Guide, Vol. 1: From Lemons to Lemonade in the New Legal Job Market* (2012)

CHAPTER 10

The Small Firm Interview

The interview. The culmination of all your research, networking, letter-writing, and pavement-pounding. Your opportunity to shine, and the employer's opportunity to determine if you're a "fit", and if you're someone with whom they want to work.

Think about it: until now, the only interaction an employer may have had with you is based on one or more sheets of paper. Your resume might *show* that you are the most qualified applicant in the pool of candidates, but small firms will *also* be evaluating you on other traits and characteristics that can only be communicated face-to-face. So, it is critical that you have a firm grasp of the fundamental and critical job interviewing techniques relevant to small firms. Before we begin, we should make clear that many of the principles that apply to other interviews also apply to small firms. So, we won't waste time here explaining …

Why you need to arrive in interview attire
Why you shouldn't text or tweet during the interview
Why it's smart to set up mock interviews beforehand with your career
    services office

There are dozens of books on interview technique at Amazon and Barnes & Noble; one we can recommend is *Guerilla Tactics for Getting the Legal Job of Your Dreams.* The author's discussion of interview techniques is comprehensive and relevant to small firms.

The Do's & Don'ts of Small Firm Interviews

By now, you already know that small firms have different hiring needs than other legal employers. So, it shouldn't surprise you that their interview style differs as well.

DO expect to interview with a panel that might include the law firm's entire staff, including administrative assistants and paralegals. Often, staff members have worked for a particular partner for many years, and their opinions are relied upon during the hiring process. At the same time, it's just as common to interview with a single attorney. Or you could be interviewing for a position at a firm with 20 attorneys, but you might actually only be working with one partner. In that case it's that partner's opinion that counts the most, if not solely. If you interview with a panel, you can be sure that they will compare notes. The smaller the law firm, the more likely they will have a "consensus" decision-making process.

DO be respectful to everyone to whom you are introduced even if they don't "officially" interview you. Assistants and paralegals often have a say in the hiring process…and they won't hesitate letting the hiring attorney know that you were rude to them while you were seated in the waiting room.

DO know your audience. Research the law firm online. If the firm is known for specific practice areas, learn what those are, what cases the firm is currently involved in, and be prepared to discuss how your skills could support those cases. Look for pending cases and learn what's going on through the courthouse Web site. Use Lexis Nexis or the West Legal Directory to find legal documents that can be attributed to a particular attorney at the firm.

DO demonstrate to your interviewer(s) that you understand the business aspect of the practice of law as well as the economic challenges facing smaller law firms. Small firms have no cushion to absorb a bad hiring decision; there is no transferring a new associate to another floor or department if there are personality conflicts. For this reason, the decision to bring on a new law clerk or associate must be assessed carefully. Make sure they know that you "get it".

DO exude confidence and enthusiasm, and answer an interviewer's questions with specific examples.

DO understand that small firm attorneys have two very important questions in mind: *Will this person fit in our office and, Can I put this person in front of a client?* You must be able to impress your interviewer(s) that you are an articulate, well-qualified professional who is enthusiastic about working for the firm.

DON'T expect lunch. For some small firms, a meal is an extravagance in time and expense.

DON'T try to force a "fit" that doesn't naturally exist. For example, if you pretend to enjoy college football because you know the partners go tailgating every weekend, you risk embarrassment when they ask what teams you follow and your opinion of the BCS rankings. By taking a more conversational approach, you will be more relaxed and able to let your own personality shine through.

DON'T whine or complain…about anything. This includes your class load, an awful professor or externship supervisor, or your last employer. Regardless how valid your complaint, it will come off as unprofessional.

DON'T inflate your skill level. Minimizing, or covering up, a lack of experience only makes it more apparent to the interviewer that you're not ready for the type of work the firm needs you to do. Being up-front and honest in a job interview is a scary proposition, but it is the best way to show you recognize your weaknesses but that you're taking steps to close the gap. Simultaneously pointing out your strong work ethic (giving concrete examples, of course), and your desire to learn, will make your inexperience much less of an issue.

DON'T ask questions about the firm's turnover (i.e., how frequently attorneys leave the firm either because they quit or were terminated). It is also wise to avoid requesting specific information about how long it takes to become partner.

DON'T forget that the interview is not over when you walk out the door. You need to debrief yourself afterward, being as critical as you can of your performance.

> Don't forget to say "thank you"…and if you interviewed with several attorneys, send a thank you to each!

Brian Hermanson, a former small firm attorney in Oklahoma, recalls one hiring experience:

> *"I recently interviewed a new group of law students [because I was trying] to determine if I was going to add a new lawyer to my office. I was…underwhelmed. I found [the students] liked to talk about what they wanted to do beyond working for me…they wanted to talk about high salaries…they generally wanted to talk about things that didn't interest me. They completely failed to do any homework to find out who I was.*

According to Hermanson, what job candidates need to know is simple:

- "Don't overvalue your services, and think you're worth more than you really are.

- "Know who's interviewing you and what they do, and what their interests are.
- "Just be open. If I'm going to hire you in my small practice, I'm going to want you to be there for a long time. You're going to be a part of my family. That being such, I don't want to hear that you want to run for [office] in three years, or that you want to work for big firm in five years, or live in a bigger city in seven years. That will shut my ears down, and I'm not going to listen to anything else. Make sure to describe to the interviewer that this is the practice for you and this is where you want to be."

What Questions You Can Expect

Why are you interested in working for a small firm?

Why don't you want to work for a big firm?

What are you looking for from your employer?

Are you used to working in a team, or can you work well independently?

Where do you see yourself in 3/5/10 years?

What ties do you have to the community?

How big is your network, and what steps would you take to expand it?

Do you consider yourself an easy person to get along with?

How do you handle yourself when you're in conflict with someone?

Tell me about a time you had to tell someone something they didn't want to hear, and how you delivered the message, and what was the outcome.

What do you like to do in your free time?

If I asked some of your peers, what do you think they would say about you?

Tell me what skills and traits you think I am looking for in a new attorney.

Tell me about a time when you had to make an unpopular decision because you knew you had to do the right thing.

What is the most significant item on your resume?

What accomplishments in your personal life have given you the most satisfaction?

Have you had much client contact experience?

How much courtroom experience do you have, and in what capacity?

How do you plan on bringing in business to the firm?

Why should we hire you?

Don't Forget to Say "Thank You"

You would think that sending a thank-you note would be a no-brainer. But so many interviewees flunk this simple (and strategic) act of courtesy. So here's the drill: your thank-you note should be received by the interviewer within 48 hours of the job interview; after that, you're at risk that someone else will have been hired…perhaps someone who took the time to send a note! Here are some other useful suggestions:

- **Make it succinct.** Don't make the mistake of drafting what is essentially another cover letter that includes skills and qualifications that you were unable to communicate during the interview. The interview is over, and trying to squeeze in more about yourself will only make you seem desperate.
- **Make it personal.** A thank-you note should thank the interviewers for their time, it should convey how much you enjoyed meeting them, and it should repeat your expression of interest in the position, and that you look forward to hearing from them in the near future.
- **Make it specific.** You should also try and bring up something specific that your interviewer said during the interview; this shows you were paying close attention to the conversation.
- **Express yourself simply.** Don't get emotional about how much you want to work for the firm, and how confident you are of being a good fit. It should have been expressed during the interview, and saying it in a thank-you note won't carry much weight.

If you interviewed with several attorneys, send a thank you to each. Don't stress too much about creating a completely different letter for each (some job-seekers feel it strange to send a similar note, if not the same note, to several attorneys at the firm, as if they would all gather in the hallway and laugh at your "form" letter). Still, it wouldn't hurt to briefly mention something specific to that interview or specific to each individual. And…not only should you send each attorney a note, but also thank any non-attorneys with whom you interviewed. Failing to do so might appear as though you feel they were less important.

Opinions differ whether to send a thank you via email or in paper form.

By all means, send email if you've been told that a hiring decision is near (within the next "few days"). Use of email is also important if you interviewed in another state, and you're concerned a stamped envelope might not reach its destination on time. Of course, the disadvantage is that everyone knows how quickly email can be drafted and sent, whereas a handwritten note requires more time and deliberation, and adds that little extra personal touch. Furthermore, handwritten notes aren't likely to be buried in an inbox or get trapped in an online server's spam filter. If you do choose to send a handwritten note, use blank, plain white stationery cards (no pictures of baby animals on the cover), and draft the note in your most legible penmanship (or, get someone to do it for you; what's the point of sending a note if the recipient cannot read it.) One more thing: do not use cards embossed with the words "Thank You" (you are not thanking someone for a birthday gift). Keep it plain and borderline boring; it means you are also keeping it professional.

When asked what advice she had for students and new graduates interested in applying to small firms, Sabrina Beavans, a small firm lawyer in New Hampshire, put it this way:

> "Be prepared for the interview. [Many of the interview questions] will be generic, but you need to practice answering them with someone. Also, the [legal job] market is so competitive right now that you should try to identify something interesting that will cause the firm to remember you. Did you study abroad? Did you volunteer on an important pro bono case?"

CHAPTER 11

The Waiting Game

When it comes to hearing back after a small firm interview, you need to be patient. Very patient. And sometimes, very, *very* patient.

Remember, the attorney who interviews you is probably the same one whose top priority is running the firm and practicing law. In fact, it is entirely possible that his or her hiring decision could be delayed for days…even weeks. As frustrating as waiting is, there is nothing you can do about a busy (and/or indecisive) small firm employer. But it is perfectly acceptable to call a week or so after the interview, and inquire if a hiring decision has been made. If it's been more than a week, you'll just have to wait. But if you continue to follow up with calls or email, it will create an impression that you're not only impatient but something of a pest.

What to do in the meantime?

Keep looking. That's right, keep looking.

By not continuing your search, you are essentially making an assumption (a hasty assumption at that) that the firm has already decided to hire you…but just hasn't gotten around to picking up the phone. Under the circumstances, it might seem odd to continue looking for a job (especially if you felt the interview went particularly well). But by putting your job search on hold, you do yourself a disservice. While you might feel you're only a phone call away from landing the job, the truth is you have no idea what is happening behind the scenes. Yes, it's possible the firm really does want to hire you, but can't because of budget constraints. Or perhaps one of the major partners wants a chance to interview you, but is out of town or in trial for the next several weeks.

Keep looking.

If you're fortunate enough to get an offer while you're still in limbo with the original firm, call and let them know you have an offer on the table. Leave your message in a voicemail or with an assistant at the firm, and give them 24 hours to return your call. If you hear nothing, assume you are no longer under consideration. No one will blame you for accepting an offer, especially if the offer you accept comes weeks (or even months) after your interview with the original firm.

Researching Salary and Benefits

If you're fortunate to get an offer, do yourself a favor: do some salary-and-benefits research before entering into negotiations. This applies whether you're a law student in search of part-time work or a summer position, or a new lawyer seeking project work or an entry-level position.

To begin, seek out your school's career development office for current rates of pay depending upon the position sought, and the firm's size and geographic area. Your school's career development staff is knowledgeable about what local firms pay law students and new, entry-level hires by virtue of their immersion in the legal job market, and having spoken to countless legal employers, and from the results of graduate employment surveys that indicate the starting salary. The staff is also likely to have a copy of an annual publication called *JD's & Jobs*. Published by NALP, it provides entry-level salaries for metropolitan areas across the country.

Another source of information is www.salary.com, where you can input factors such as "Atlanta", "small law firm," and "law clerk", and get hourly rates of pay or a specific salary range. Note: salary information for smaller job markets is less likely to be available. Yet another resource is a Job Seekers Salary Calculator at the Web site for the National Association of Colleges and Employers (www.jobsearchintelligence.com/NACE/jobseekers/salary-calculator.php#). Their salary calculator filters information by state, region, occupation, years of education, and level of experience

Armed with potential rates of compensation, it's important that you negotiate in terms of a salary "range" rather than a set rate. A range is more palatable because it is much less awkward for an employer to slide within a stated range than it is to suggest a lower (or higher!) amount from one set number. Example: the firm's partner asks you what rate of pay you have in mind. He's prepared to pay you $25/hour, but you say $20/hour...which means you've left money on the table. Or the reverse. The employer is prepared to pay $15/hour, but you ask for $20/hour. An awkward moment for both parties.

Instead, negotiate in terms of a salary range. It's easier for both parties to close the gap. Based on your salary-and-benefits research, you might say something like: ...

"Given the market value of comparable positions in similarly-sized firms in this city, and considering my background, I would anticipate the salary range to be $x to $x."

Or perhaps you keep the door open without mentioning a salary range. As in …

"I'm feeling really optimistic about this position. I'm open to considering any offer you might wish to make because I'm confident that you will want to fairly compensate me based upon the market rate and my skills and experience."

For Law Students: Negotiating Salaries/Hourly Rates

As a law student, you should be versed in the two rates that apply to you specifically: hourly rates for project work, and salaries for full-time summer employment.

After you've gotten an idea of typical hourly rates for your geographic area and firm size, you can go into negotiations well-prepared. Share with the attorney what sources you used to derive the range of rates you are proposing. This is especially important when you are working with an attorney who has never hired a part-time law clerk or summer associate before, and who thinks that paying a clerk more than $5/hour is highway robbery. Letting the attorney know that you did not pull your numbers out of a hat will make it much more likely that he/she will find your numbers credible. You may also want to let the employer know that your career resource office has salary data that they would be willing to share.

Note: it is *your* responsibility to establish the terms of employment with a potential employer prior to beginning work. Establishing terms at the onset generally reduces the possibility of misunderstandings or conflicts during, and at the completion, of your employment. As a law student, it is especially important that you clearly understand how much time the attorney has allotted to complete the project you are being assigned. You should also be knowledgeable of any employer-provided research tools (such as commercial online databases for legal research) to which you may have access. Do not make the mistake of using your law school Westlaw or Lexis accounts do to work for private firms. It violates the terms of use.

Also know that there are many factors that can affect what a small firm employer is willing and able to pay for project work, including:

- *Geographic location.* Hourly rates for small firms in Minneapolis are obviously greater than at small law firms in rural Iowa.

- *Firm size.* A partnership that consists of two general practitioners will generally not be able to support as high an hourly rate as, say, a midsized firm that has 30 attorneys.
- *Practice areas.* Boutique law firms that focus on a specific practice area will typically seek out more "senior" law students who have taken specialized classes, clinics and externships, or have practical work experience. In other words, specialized knowledge often warrants higher rates of pay. Be mindful, though, that rates can vary significantly between practice areas: for example, a student on track to achieve a certificate in law, science, and technology can probably demand a higher project rate than one who has a specialization in family law.

But what do you do if you're offered less than what you believe is an acceptable salary range? It would be easy to feel slighted, insulted, even indignant. But there could be another explanation. It's possible the attorney is not being cheap; he or she may have a cash-flow problem. You could decide to accept a lower rate because you feel the work will lead to bigger and better things…or that you have a chance to really impress the attorney with your work product and efficiency, making it likely that you will be asked to work on another assignment, then another, and so on. The ball is in your court. The job may represent a great couple of lines on your resume, a solid reference and future contact, exposure to a real-life set of facts and circumstances, and a chance to problem-solve.

Is it worth losing all of that over a few bucks an hour?

For New Attorneys: Salary Negotiations

Affordable billing rates are what set most small firms apart from Biglaw. As a consequence of less expensive rates, new attorneys should expect small firm salaries to be commensurate with that business model. *In short, most small firms cannot (and will not) compete with large firm salaries.* And yet when it comes to negotiations, smaller firms usually have more flexibility than large firms or government agencies, and are often willing to discuss alternative compensation plans that differ from the traditional flat annual salary because they realize a new lawyer's revenue will probably not be enough to cover her salary. So, be flexible in terms of your salary or hourly rate arrangement; it could mean the difference between closing the deal and not.

An equity partner in one small firm put it this way:

"If someone tells me they want 100k, I want to hear them say, 'I've been a member of this community, and my family's been a member, for the last 60

years, and I've been a part of this organization, and I've got deals with such-and-such businesses and I expect them all to be clients, and I expect to bring in x thousands of dollars of revenue annually. Plus...I'm willing to work at least 2,000 hours a year. I know you will bill me out at $200/hour, and having calculated what profit will [make for the firm], I think I'm a bargain at 100k'. That would impress me. That would tell me this is a serious person who understands what it takes to be successful as a young lawyer in a small law firm."

The two most important factors that will affect your salary are:

Your productivity level. Some small firms offer a lower annual salary but provide a bonus if you bill more than a certain number of hours per month, per quarter, or per year. If the firm does offer a bonus, ask if it is discretionary or automatic. If some cases, your level of productivity is not based on your total billable hours but rather as a net of the difference between what is collected and what has to be written off. So, if you have more than a significant amount of billable hours that were "re-do's," or if you happened to do work for a dead-beat client, your perceived bonus could go from lucrative to non-existent.

Your rainmaking skills. The ability to bring in new business (make it rain) can put you in a great position to negotiate. In fact, it's quite possible—but you can't assume—that the firm will give you a share of the fees generated by any client you bring in. But firms calculate shared fees differently. For some, sharing fees depends on whether you or someone else in the firm does the work. For example, a firm might offer a 33 percent shared fee for clients you brought in if you do the work, but only 20 percent if another attorney does the work.

You might also be able to negotiate for some deferred compensation and other benefits. For example:

Retirement or pension plan. Some law firms have a straight pension plan. If so, find out when the pension vests (when you achieve ownership/rights to all the funds in the pension including contributions made by the firm), and the amounts of the employer's contributions to the plan. You might also inquire about the firm's contributions to a 401(k) Plan or IRA.

Medical benefits. Find out what exactly is covered (i.e., medical, dental, optical), and the amount of the deductible and co-payments. If you have dependents, find out if they are covered and at what cost.

Life insurance and disability. Some employers provide life insurance and disability insurance.

Parking fees. This might seem trivial, but in some offices (especially those located in major cities), the monthly fee can easily run several hundreds of dollars a month to park your car in a structure attached to the building.

Bar review course fees & moving expenses.

Annual bar dues. Find out about associations other than your own mandatory state bar dues which are, in fact, normally covered by the firm. Dues for other types of associations like the ABA, county or city bar associations and the like, can add up quickly. Section memberships within your state bar might also be covered by the firm especially if it is for an area in which you are actively practicing (e.g, State Bar Environmental Law section).

CLE seminars. Many states require bar members to satisfy a CLE requirement. These, too can add up if you consider a single, one hour CLE seminar can run $50 depending on the locale.

Vacation and sick time. Determine how many weeks of vacation and sick leave you can accrue per year and when you can use them.

Maternity-paternity/family leave. Policies vary and sometimes include an unpaid leave component (six weeks paid, six weeks unpaid).

A few other considerations:

In any negotiation with the employer, remember you are entering into a long-term working relationship. Be mindful that the decision to hire any new associate will be costly to the firm in terms of salary and training for the first few years. And that whatever concession you push for, might ultimately affect your working relationship. Therefore, your goal should be to creatively meet the needs of *both* you and your employer (think win-win) without "costing" the employer an additional cash outlay. If work-life balance becomes important to you early in your career, you might be able to negotiate a more flexible working arrangement. But it should only be asked for after demonstrating at least a few years of commitment and profitability to the firm. If you were to bring up the subject of a flexible working arrangement during salary negotiations, it would demonstrate that you don't understand small firm dynamics, and this would not be received well.

The Upside (and Downside) of Volunteering

With so many Biglaw layoffs in recent years (nearly 10,000 since 2008), and with thousands of new lawyers just entering the legal job market, it's easy to understand why volunteering is so popular. In times of a prolonged recession, volunteering is a smart way to gain exposure to potential employers. This is especially true if you're trying to break into a specialized area of law only practiced by very seasoned attorneys (e.g., capital defense, land use, zoning). *It's our opinion, that even though small firms are skeptical of hiring someone with little or no experience, that you should work for free only for a very short period of time, and only if there is truly no other way to get your foot in the door of the firm you are targeting.* Instead of offering to volunteer from the start, we suggest that you propose to do a project for a very low hourly rate (something just above minimum wage), and tell the attorney that you can negotiate a higher rate for the next project if he or she likes your work. Offering to work for free might give the attorney a bad impression of how much you think your work is worth.

One problem with volunteering is that it might collide with the Fair Labor Standards Act (FLSA), which requires for-profit companies (which includes private law firms) to pay every employee at least minimum wage.

If any private sector employer suggests that you volunteer or perform work for less than minimum wage, you need to be aware that the U.S. Department of Labor issued a Fact Sheet in April 2010 regarding the issue of the Fair Labor Standards Act and uncompensated interns. As a job seeker, it would be beneficial for you to be aware of this regulation because it's quite possible an attorney or firm may not realize that asking you to volunteer is a violation of the FLSA. If you find yourself in this situation, it's not a good idea to wave a copy of the Act in the employer's face. The more sensible approach would be to casually (and calmly) tell the attorney that it's your understanding that the Department of Labor prevents you from working for free unless it is in an internship situation. If after being reminded on the FLSA requirements, the attorney is still unwilling to pay at least minimum wage, you can always ask him/her whether the experience will meet the requirements for an unpaid internship. If not, it's up to you to decide whether or not the experience is worth it.

SECTION III
WELCOME TO THE FIRM

CHAPTER 12

A Day in the Life

Practicing law involves daily interaction with individuals undergoing stressful, highly charged experiences. One day you might be working with a client who lost his job; the next day you're sitting across from someone facing foreclosure or bankruptcy...or someone whose family member was jailed or had died. For the newer attorney, these situations will unleash a whirlwind of emotions that need to be sorted through. Observe how others in your office conduct themselves and, if you are unsure about protocol or expectations, just ask.

To hear associate Amy Bokor tell it, a day in the life of an attorney is nothing like what the media prepares you for.

> *"Never watch another legal show on TV again," she says. "Real life law practice is NOTHING like how television portrays law firms. It's not sexy, it's not glamorous. It is a lot of hard work and long hours. Be prepared to think about your cases in the shower, driving to the grocery store, in the middle of the night, and even when you're on vacation."*

And the life of a newer attorney presents a steep learning curve.

> *"The learning curve [at your new firm] will be difficult. You will have to learn to research, write, and identify issues, as well as manage your time, your client expectations, the firm's revenue expectations, and any interactions with difficult and unresponsive opponents. Always keep in mind that your reputation and integrity will be the most important factors in your long term success."*
> —KEITH (CLASS OF 2003)

Or this observation from Joseph (Class of 2007) in Salt Lake City:

> *"You need to realize that you chose a profession where you do not get to set your schedule. The court does, the client does, your deadlines do. So, decide right now to do what it takes to get the job done. Forty hours a week is for suckers*

and union members. We [lawyers] work a lot…so deal with it. That doesn't mean that you get to be grouchy, or drink too much, or do drugs, or have family problems. You made the decision to be a lawyer, so suck it up and quite whining. There are lots of people who would love to have our education, our jobs, and our salaries."

And even as you learn about substantive law, it's just as important to interact well with the firm's office staff. Many new attorneys commit a serious error in judgment by undervaluing or even disrespecting the support staff. One small firm associate in South Carolina put it this way:

"Get to know and respect the legal assistants and paralegals. They can be your biggest ally or the worst impediment to your career. Many new attorneys have little or no respect for staff, legal assistants and paralegals. It's important to remember that these individuals have been working for lawyers for many years, and probably know much, much more about the practice of law than the new attorney."

Another point on interoffice dynamics is relevant here:

Don't be too quick to take things personally if a co-worker snaps at you. A law office can be an emotionally charged environment when you take into account the heavy workload and the range of client issues. It could also be that your co-workers are dealing with personal, financial, economic, or life-changing pressures that impact their moods or behavior. Be mindful that you are doing your best effort to produce high-quality work so let the moment pass and move on. *Change is inevitable, but drama is a choice.* Attitude is paramount to helping you to adjust in your new role. If you approach each day optimistically…as a new opportunity to learn…your enthusiasm will be contagious, and the other attorneys and staff around you will be far more willing to offer help and support. Remember, it is expected that you will have more questions than answers at this stage of your career. Associate Joseph McAllister wants you to know that, *"It gets easier as you figure out what you are doing."*

Is there a typical work day? In a word, no. It varies by practice area. If you are a litigator in the weeks leading up to trial, what is typical for you is atypical for an estate planning attorney. Associate Kassie Doyle reports that while she was learning how to practice Admiralty and Maritime law her typical work-day was 9 to 6:30 with a full Saturday thrown in once or twice a month, in addition to taking research home to review. Associate Brett Lieberman says his workday is from 9 to 6, but that he almost never leaves before 7 p.m. He doesn't work weekends, but at home he *frequently* works into the night via remote access.

What is typical is that as a new lawyer trying to learn about substantive areas and absorb how to practice law, you will be putting in longer hours at first, until you learn how to work more efficiently and effectively. Do not develop a reputation for being the first attorney out the door. You need to be committed to doing what it will take to succeed, recognizing that the time that you initially put in will make you a great lawyer.

The Billable Hour

Black's Law Dictionary defines a billable hour as a unit of time used by an attorney to account for work performed and chargeable to a client. Most often, time is recorded in increments of six or 10 minutes, and clients are billed for the hours worked multiplied by the lawyer's hourly rate.

A firm's revenue is almost solely dependent upon billable hours.

The concept seems simple enough, but takes a little getting used to.

During this economic downturn, clients are balking at paying for all the work done on their behalf, and the notion of what is *billable* and what is *non-billable* (i.e. written off by the firm), has become a point of contention. You are new to the practice of law. You probably know little or nothing about insurance law, and yet you are called upon to research and draft a document about an insurance law issue. There is a certain amount of "getting up to speed" on the topic that is implied when a new associate begins, but the client will not want to pay for educating you on their case or subject. Therefore, the firm must write off some of your non-billable time as you learn about insurance law. The clear expectation is that your non-billables will decrease with time as you gain experience. Which leads us to a formula known as the realization rate. This calculates the difference between your recorded time and the percentage of that time paid for by the client. For example, if you logged nine hours at work per day, but only 4.5 of those nine hours could be billed to clients, your realization rate is only 50 percent. This number might be tolerated when you are new, but if you want to become of greater value to the firm you need to improve your realization rate.

How many billable hours are expected? As recently as 2009, Biglaw firms with 250 or more attorneys expected them to bill almost 2,100 hours per year (although that number is in flux given the state of the economy and client shrinkage). Smaller firms have somewhat less demanding expectations. Most of the small firm associates we contacted in smaller cities (Charlotte, Atlanta, Salt Lake City, Seattle) said they were expected to bill 1,800 to 1,850 hours a year, and even that was not strictly enforced. For a more detailed discussion of billable hours, consult a 2011 study conducted by NALP (http://www.nalp.org/assoc_hrs_feb2011).

What does this mean to you?

If you're at work 40 hours a week for 50 weeks, it comes to 2,000 working hours. But "at work" hours don't translate into "billable" hours. It is generally accepted that about one third of an attorney's hours are nonbillable. This means that to yield 2,000 billable hours requires about 2,600 work hours, which includes such nonbillable activities as involvement in specialty or local bar associations, mandatory CLE's, and any committee work you might perform. At least these nonbillables are more productive, though. They have the potential to generate referrals and bring in new clients.

Tracking billable hours. Like all law firms, yours will have a billing system in place. Understanding the nuances of how it works is a top priority.

Most firms bill in six or 10 minute increments, so you must jot down every phone call, log in each piece of correspondence, and make a record of each time you work on a client's file. If you're not fastidious about logging ALL of your time every day (billable and non-billable hours) your firm will lose revenue. As you get started, you may find it helpful to keep a notebook by your phone to record how your time was spent. At the end of the day, those notes will help you enter the results into the firm's timekeeping system. The key to accuracy is to devise a note-keeping system that works for you and the firm.

- For a *single entry,* you might enter *".30 hour - attended 341 hearing for Davis case".*
- For a *block entry,* you might enter *"2.5 hours - Bowen case: created inventory log, reviewed file, prepared client, attended 341 hearing, met with trustee to coordinate asset viewing of farm equipment."*

While you're still new to time-keeping, it is usually helpful to use too much detail than try to recall specifics when the client bills are generated at the end of the month. This may seem awkward at first because most of us are not conditioned to think of our workday in six- or 10-minute increments. But in the life of a law firm—Biglaw or smaller firm—it is imperative to account for all of your time, even if you are concerned that you may have spent too much time researching a particular topic or drafting a document. This information provides the firm with the means to assess your work product, and whether they wish to expend further resources on this project.

> Accurately record your time and never inflate or pad your client billing time. Your reputation is at stake.

Note: In recent years, as the cost of legal services has surged, the billable hour has come under attack. In a preface to the 2002 ABA Commission Report on the Billable Hour, then-ABA President Robert Hirshon wrote, "The billable hour is fundamentally about quantity over quality, repetition over creativity. With no gauge for intangibles such as productivity, knowledge or technological advancements, the billable hour model is a counter-intuitive measure of value. For further discussion, read Jessika Ferm's blog post, *The Billable Hour Zombie: Why You Need to Act Now to Avoid an Attack on Your Business* (ABA's Law Practice Management blog, July 2011).

How **collectible** *hours differ from billable hours.* For many small firms, greater emphasis is placed on the amount of *collectible* hours rather than billable hours. The reality of small firm economics is that they simply don't have sufficient capital reserves to let bills go uncollected for very long. So, the ability to actually collect the fees for the time they bill is far more critical than the billable hour itself. Collectible hours are distinguished from billable hours in another way, too. It's important to point out, that in many smaller law firms there is an expectation that the attorneys will be involved in the collection of their client's bills. In Biglaw, this is a function of an Accounts Receivable Department. Smaller firms don't have the luxury of such departments, so this additional responsibility will quickly train you in Billing 101. And—as you begin taking client questions about their bill—it will increase your awareness and sensitivity to time-keeping. **Note:** some small firms have an annual dollar range of expected collectibles that they will discuss with you during the interview.

What Value-Added Means to You

Regardless of size, law firms live and die by two variables: how much they bill and collect from clients, and how well they control overhead (salaries, rent, electricity, telephone, broadband, malpractice insurance, advertising, etc.). Dwane Cates, founder and managing partner of a three-attorney firm in Phoenix, explains:

> *"We run on a really, really tight budget. We're not rolling in money but we do OK, and I'm the engine that drives the firm. I also do all the marketing. Because of that, I need to hire a new attorney who will allow me to do more on that*

front. In other words, I need new attorneys to take the low-level stuff off my plate so that I can do more rainmaking."

As a law student, nearly every waking hour for three years was once devoted to your learning how to think like and practice like a lawyer. Now, as an employee of a small firm, the focus shifts to learning the "business" of law. You must learn how your presence at the firm affects the bottom line, and how every hour spent training you…and not billing for that time…equates to lost revenues. But even if you have the lowest billing rate in the firm, you are most valuable when you are helping the partner(s) maximize their time…which is billed at the highest rate…so they can provide outstanding client service.

So, how can you make yourself valuable?

- Go to conferences and trade meetings on behalf of the firm
- Follow up with clients about their bills
- Offer to make collection phone calls and providing friendly reminders when needed
- Network in the business community
- Offer to teach seminars to trade groups as a way to put the firm's name out there
- Make sure the firm's clients believe they are getting value for their money
- Use cost-effective research methods; don't automatically log onto premium online legal research first without thinking through your issue
- Learn the per-minute cost of your firm's subscription-based services
- Learn if your state bar offers cost-effective research options like FastCase or LoisLaw
- Check on the availability of a treatise or book that can provide the big picture before researching online

Associate Brett Liebermann speaks to this value-added proposition:

"I believe I add value to my firm by ensuring that my memoranda is in a highly usable format. That my analysis is so well-reasoned that the partners can insert it into their document and apply the facts. In fact, to make their life as easy as possible, I often repeat complete cites (rather than using id or ibid), sentence after sentence, so the partners can lift separate sentences without returning to the previous sentence to rewrite the full cite. These are some of the little things I can do to make it easier for the partners who are working on big cases, and whose hourly rate is almost double my own. If I can cut down on the time they

spend in the trenches, they are free to meet and sign up new clients. This means they can bring more business…which means I get more business."

Joseph D. McAllister, a third-year associate, says that in his experience some junior associates tend to sit back and wait for work to come to them.

"A new associate should learn that there are some things a managing partner has to handle, but there are other things that the associate can offer to do for the partners. Essentially, be a problem-solver. Find problems and solve them, or try to help solve them. The problem with many associates is that they sit back and wait for work to come to them, and then they wait for the praise or rewards. This does not work. An associate needs to take charge of their situation, and find tasks that they can do to help out the firm."

IN THEIR OWN WORDS

Q: What should new attorneys know about the realities of small firm practice?

"The learning curve [at your new firm] will be difficult. You will have to learn to research, write, and identify issues, as well as manage your time, your client expectations, the firm's revenue expectations, and any interactions with difficult and unresponsive opponents. Always keep in mind that your reputation and integrity will be the most important factors in your long term success." —KEITH (CLASS OF 2003)

"Make sure the attorneys [at your firm] know that you have a fire to learn, and that you want to become a better attorney. That way, they will spend more time with you. [In fact], the more time you spend with an experienced attorney the quicker you will become one." —TROY (CLASS OF 2010)

"Turn off your television, and NEVER watch another legal show again. Real life law practice is NOTHING like how TV portrays it. It's not sexy or glamorous; it's a lot of hard work and long hours. Be prepared to think about your cases in the shower, driving to the grocery store, in the middle of the night, and even when you're on a well-deserved vacation." —AMY (CLASS OF 2006)

"To be completely honest, my first year of practice was all about finding a way to be comfortable with the fact that I really had no idea what I was doing. On most days, I felt like I was playing dress-up. Slowly, however, I discovered that

I was becoming more knowledgeable and comfortable. Law school provides you with many of the skills to be a successful lawyer, but only day-to-day practice can make you good at your job." —Lisa (Class of 2008)

"Work [at small firms] can be time-consuming and intense. You need to take care of yourself (both physically and emotionally). If you neglect yourself (too little sleep, no exercise, poor diet), it will show up in some form in your work)."
—Nikki (Class of 2009)

"Get to know and respect the legal assistants and paralegals. They can be your biggest ally or worst impediment to your career. Many new attorneys have little or no respect for staff, legal assistants and paralegals. It's important to remember that these individuals have been working for lawyers for many years, and probably know much, much more about the practice of law than the new attorney." —Adam (Class of 2006)

"You should talk with your legal assistant, paralegal, senior associates, and partners regularly. Don't be afraid to bug people, even when they seem busy. If you have a concern about a case, raise it. But spend some time planning for these conversations so they are focused, to the point, and concise."
—Shelly (Class of 2007)

"You need to realize that you chose a profession where you do not get to set your schedule. The court does, the client does, your deadlines do. So, decide right now to do what it takes to get the job done. Forty hours a week is for suckers and union members. We [lawyers] work a lot… so deal with it. That doesn't mean that you get to be grouchy, or drink too much, or do drugs, or have family problems. You made the decision to be a lawyer, so suck it up and quite whining. There are lots of people who would love to have our education, our jobs, and our salaries. But, the most important thing is this: always be prepared! You may not be the smartest attorney in the courtroom, or have the most experience, or the most polished style, but always commit to your clients that you will be the most prepared. Make sure that when you go into the courtroom, or into a negotiation, you know everything there is to know about the case and the law. Because when two qualified attorneys disagree about the law, the one who is most prepared usually wins. Plus, your bosses will appreciate having someone by their side who knows everything about the case, and can whisper it in their ear, or back them up on a disputed point."
—Joseph (Class of 2007)

"[New] attorneys need to have definite instruction on trust accounting and banking. This is by far the main reason why many attorneys get in trouble with the [state] Bar. Appropriate attention should be given to this in law school, and every law student should be required to take a course on fiduciary duties, basic bank account, and trust fund management." —ADAM (CLASS OF 2006)

"I wish that I had known how to talk to clients about money. I was completely unprepared to deal with collecting fees, and I had no idea how to value a case, whether to charge a flat fee or retainer, or how to work with clients who might need payments plans. These decisions were left up to me, but I had never been exposed to it before." —KATHRYN (CLASS OF 2010)

CHAPTER 13

Meet an Associate

After providing a composite view of "A Day in the Life," we offer a snapshot of one senior associate who provides a more seasoned perspective:

Sabrina C. Beavens

Education: Stetson University College of Law (Class of 2002)

Resume: Practicing law for 9 years

Practice specialty: Foreclosure litigation, bankruptcy, creditors' rights, business law and litigation

Q: Why did you decide to go into small firm practice?

A: "The opportunity to work on substantive matters and issues on a case (compared to document reviews and performing legal research) earlier in my career…less strict billable hour requirements…and the ability to try several areas of practice before deciding what areas would ultimately become my focus. I think it is important for new attorneys to have an honest conversation with themselves as to what will make them happy. *For me, I knew I did not want to be married to my firm.* I enjoy practicing law, especially when cases present new legal issues or challenges. I also enjoy turning off my lawyer button and spending time with my family and friends and pursuing my hobbies."

Q: What did you know about small firm practice beforehand?

A: "[There are] fewer billable hours, associates earn less salary [than in Biglaw], and new attorneys are given more responsibility faster."

Q: What do you enjoy about small firm practice?

A: "The simplicity of a small practice. There are no politics, and the attorneys share a common vision for our firm. We work as a team with a focus on doing great work for our clients, and not on self-promotion. When I hear my friends describe being on this committee or that committee at their firm, our practice feels like a firm and not a corporation. [Of course], not all small firms operate in this manner, so new attorneys should ask questions at their interview to try to ferret out this issue. For example, you need to be careful in family-owned firms. They may be a good place to spend a few years of practicing, but in the long run it may be challenging to move up to partnership."

Q: What legal or practice skills were you least prepared for?
A: "Interacting with real clients with real problems is difficult. They will grab onto any hope you give them, so you must be careful with the words you choose. When telling someone that their worst-case scenario is a possibility, it's tempting to soften the message. But I find that you need to be direct with clients, and then help them develop a strategy to deal with their problems. Also, [the subject of] fees is a challenge. Even on contingency fee cases where the agreed percentage did not seem like a problem to the client at the start of the case, many clients will challenge [you] when the case is settled."

Q: What would you tell a roomful of 3L's/new grads about small firm practice?
A: "Law school is the perfect time to evaluate what type of firm fits you best. If you think a small firm is better, find out what firms bring in associates to develop them as lawyers and not just billable hour machines. Find a firm where you think you will fit in. There is nothing worse than going to work every day to somewhere where you do not feel comfortable. And do not make the decision solely based on salary. When you find the right firm, be prepared to work hard. Just because there is not a strict billable hour requirement does not mean that hard work is not required. Client demands and case deadlines exist regardless of a billable hour requirement. Also, be prepared to pitch in on the less glamorous work when preparing for a big hearing or trial. I would also tell a roomful of 3L's to be in control of their own careers. No one will do it for you. You have to develop your contacts and put the time in on Bar Association committees if you expect to someday be asked to be in a position of leadership. You must identify speaking opportunities and seek them out."

Q: What are a new lawyer's three biggest challenges?
A: 1) "Usually you do not report to just one partner, and the partners probably do not coordinate the assignments. So, most partners appreciate it when a new lawyer brings competing deadlines to their attention, and then asks for help in prioritizing the work.
2) "Balancing billable and non-billable work. Depending on how small the firm is, the number of staff may not make someone available to take care of

such non-billable work as doing the mail or making copies for hearings. A new lawyer must learn to be self-sufficient, because the reality is that staff time will be delegated first to senior associates and partners. Also, while it is important to get involved in Bar Association committees, a new lawyer must be mindful of how much time they are volunteering. I found that you gain more respect from Bar leadership for the quality of your contributions rather than the quantity (and it is more manageable to keep billable hours at a respectable amount).

3) "If a new lawyer has aspirations of ever developing their own practice—either within that small firm or going solo—it's important to develop marketing strategies even as you come out of law school. Maintain your law school contacts, and begin to build new contacts among legal and business professionals. Marketing is an ongoing process in a small firm, and the sooner you build the foundation the better."

Q: What are some mistakes commonly made by new lawyers?

A: "One is overconfidence. There is no substitute for experience even if you are the top of your class, law review, etc. Another common mistake is undervaluing the Bar Associations, especially the Young Lawyers Committees. They give you a chance to talk about practice issues you may not feel comfortable asking in front of more experienced lawyers. And it is nice to know that you are not the only one who didn't know how to do "X". Also, the Young Lawyers Committees tend to be active in community events which are fun, they provide an opportunity to meet other lawyers, and they provide a public service. And another [common mistake] is not finding a mentor. Whether it is a senior lawyer in your practice, or a lawyer you met at a Bar event, a mentor is a huge resource for a new lawyers."

Q: What can a newer associate do to "add value" to the firm?

A: "Volunteer to help with projects geared toward getting new clients, such as helping a partner write for a publication or prepare for a presentation."

Q: What advice have you for students and grads interested in applying to small firms?

A: "Be prepared for the interview. [Many of the interview questions] will be generic, but you need to practice answering them with someone. Also, the [legal job] market is so competitive right now that you should try to identify something interesting that will cause the firm to remember you. Did you study abroad? Did you volunteer on an important pro bono case?"

CHAPTER 14

Meet the Partners

After reading about the experiences of several associates (in chapters 12 and 13, and throughout the book), this chapter offers the perspectives of a few small firm partners, who identify what really matters to them and what they want you to know to succeed in small firm practice:

On Networking
By Danny Ortega (partner), The Ortega Law Firm, Phoenix AZ

"Networking by itself means nothing. But networking combined with showing who you are as an individual, and as a contributing member of the community, is extremely important.

How do you show people who you are? You just get out there. Volunteer anywhere, because you don't know who the lawyer in the crowd is. If you're [volunteering] because something is meaningful to you, that you are passionate about, and someone sees that in you, you're going to attract attention. I met a law student recently who asked me to lunch. She says, 'I'm interested in doing some work for you.' I tell her that we're not hiring right now, but let's talk and go from there. One day I get in a bind and I need some research done. So, I pick up the phone and call this person. Since then I've hired her three different times. Everything I've ever garnered in my career has been out of relationships that I've had with people. I can't emphasize more that if you spend all of your time in law school doing nothing but studying, you are limiting yourself to a small number of opportunities. Hiding out [in law school] is going to be a liability. But I urge you to stick with your interests. Do things that are natural to you. When you sit down with someone that you might have an interest in working for, don't think about it as though you're just having a chat; think about it as if you're interviewing for a job even if you're not!"

On Getting Hired
By Carolyn Oberholtzer (partner), The Rose Law Group, Scottsdale AZ

"Small firms don't like to date. We want to know you beforehand.

I don't think small firms hire attorneys that they don't already know in some way. So it's very important during your 2nd and 3rd years [of law school] to be forming relationships with small firms. You might not get a job with that firm, but anyone who's worked with our firm, we work hard to find them a job. And that's the thing: you want as many allies [as possible] to be looking for jobs for you. If you only have four hours per week to give, and you target small firms, find one commonality between you and someone else, and say, 'I have four hours to give you to do some research'. That's a great way to get into a firm. Everyone we have ever hired was someone who clerked for us before taking the Bar. Some of those positions were very brief, like contract work. But we generally bring those people in. [After all], why would we look anywhere else? If we've got a law clerk who proved themselves, and who is doing good work, and who is making us happy, that's the person we are going to hire if we need somebody that fall or after the Bar. Sometimes the timing [allows] us to hire that person long term. For small firms everything is about timing. Sometimes you just have to be in the right place at the right time when you're asking small firms for work."

By Randy Nussbaum (Shareholder), Nussbaum, Gillis & Dinner, Scottsdale AZ

"Almost all hiring in small firms is based on relationships and networking, for the simple fact we work closely together. This is why small firms almost always hire people they already know and trust. Small firm attorneys want to be reassured the new hire has strong social skills, and in many cases, a sense of humor. That is why younger lawyers looking for work [should] join a local bar association, and get themselves known by lawyers in the community. [The thinking is] if you know someone, you already know what his/her personality is like when you are considering them for employment. Knowing that ahead of time makes it much more likely I will hire that person."

By Carolyn Oberholtzer

"At a small firm, you are always [asking yourself], *'Am I busy enough to justify hiring another person?'* You have to be super-busy for an extended period of time to say, *'Alright, I am now busy enough to justify hiring, so it's time to look.'* But it's because I am so busy that I don't have time to look, and posting jobs is expensive and time-consuming. So, I usually blast an email [to colleagues], and say, *'Here's what we need. Who knows someone to help with this situation?'* When you target small firms, bypass HR. If you want to make individual contact with a lawyer, call the lawyer. Send a brief email…without typos! Be careful emailing your resume around, though. Law firms have spam filters. But if there's a firm you really want to notice you, send a paper resume. I get a paper resume once per year and it can make a big difference. If [after all that] you don't hear back, follow up with a phone call. If someone called and said, *'You know all this stuff about this area, I see you've been doing it for 15 years, I'd like to talk to you for a few minutes and pick your brain.'* The ego in you says, *'Oh, someone feels like I know something. I'm going to call them back.'"*

The Job Search
By Randy Nussbaum (Shareholder), Nussbaum, Gillis & Dinner, Scottsdale AZ

"It is crucial for job-seekers to know the folks with whom they're interviewing, and to find some way to immediately relate to that person in a natural way. I recently interviewed a young woman for an associate position, and her resume indicated that she was interested in world history. Being a history buff myself, I wanted to learn more about her. So, I asked her to tell me about the most recent book she had read. As she began talking, I kept waiting for her to demonstrate some enthusiasm but it never came, and the longer she spoke the more I realized she would never fit in my firm. If she wasn't able to muster up some excitement on a topic she is purportedly interested in, I have to assume that she is generally a more stoic kind of person. That might fit at other firms but not ours."

Communicating with Partners
By Kevin Johnson (partner), Thompson Sizemore Gonzalez & Hearing,
Tampa FL

"When you go into a partner with a question, the first thing they want to know is: where are you on this? What have you identified? How are you asking the question? The second thing they want to know is: what is your tentative answer right now? I don't want you to come in and say, *'How do I do this'*? It shows that you aren't putting any effort into it. What I want to see is how you have set up the question, what you think goes into the question, what you think the answer is. Then I will ask you what you have looked at so far. Have you looked at this case? Have you thought about this fact? I want to see how you are blending the facts with the available case log. That's what it's all about, integrating the two. So, then I will talk to you a little bit, and figure out that you are missing some key facts. And I will say, *'Well, why don't you go back and think about this set of facts and see how that approach shapes things.'* Or, *'You really need to go read this case, and maybe that will change the answer you are coming up with.'* If you can't convince the partner that you are right, you're not going to be able to convince the judge. [So the partner] pokes and prods, trying to determine if you have everything figured out. If you do, that's great. If you don't, [the partner] is going to try to find what you're missing, because they don't want to be the one to take an argument in front of the judge and have the judge pull the plug on us."

By Camille Iurillo (founding partner), Iurillo & Associates, St. Petersburg FL

"The way you communicate with the partner is also very important.

It isn't enough to write a memo about what your research shows, and then hand it to them. The partner may want a formal memo, they may want an informal memo, or they may just want you to talk about it with them. You need to find out what format they prefer. You can usually clarify this with other associates. But it is not a matter of just handing the partner a memo. It's being able to communicate about the case log, working through your argument, understanding the law…and then being able to brainstorm with the lawyer with whom you're working. That's really important. It means you know your stuff better than just writing it down. If I can cut and paste [your memo], you've done your work. But some of the associate's arguments aren't that good. Being able to write that argument the way I will present it to the judge, or close enough to where I'm just tweaking it, is very important. But sometimes, in the beginning, it's the hardest part for young associates. They find the law, but spinning the argument to apply to law is important."

By Randy Nussbaum (Shareholder), Nussbaum, Gillis & Dinner, Scottsdale AZ

"Convince the partner from the moment you first meet that person that you are the type who will seek out work before being asked. This issue drives me nuts [because] time and time again I have to go to lawyers and ask if they are busy."

How Associates Can Add Value
By Kevin Johnson (partner), Thompson Sizemore Gonzalez & Hearing, Tampa FL

"The first thing I would tell a young associate at our firm is to expect to work hard. There are a lot of people out there who work hard, who can give 2,200 hours if that's what is needed. But there's a difference between just giving 2,200 hours and working efficiently in that 2,200 hours. It's the same unit of time, but if you can move a lot more cases in that 2,200 hours—and you're not spinning the wheels on one case—then you are more effective. And if you are not only a hard worker but an efficient worker, then you can also figure out when to work on things, and what to bring back that will add that extra value.

That's what really separates a good associate from an associate who is just a hard worker. And you have to understand that in this profession, hard work is sort of the floor. It's what is expected of us when we go into [law]."

By Randy Nussbaum (shareholder), Nussbaum, Gillis & Dinner, Scottsdale AZ

"I really appreciate when our younger lawyers network with lawyers from larger firms, and even introduce me to those lawyers. This interaction helps build firm visibility and shows pride in the firm. I also love it when a younger lawyer brings me information which demonstrates that they are more than a 9 to 5 robot. For example, I really appreciate it when a younger lawyer comes up with a marketing or management idea which does not put money in the lawyer's pocket, but may improve the firm generally."

On Work-Life Balance

By Camille Iurillo (founding partner), Iurillo & Associates, St. Petersburg FL

"My firm is a smaller firm. It's me and two associates, two paralegals, and three staff. I try to encourage new people not to work late or on weekends. But when we're getting ready for trial, the associates and I are trying to think of every issue. It's just issue, issue, issue. Have you addressed this issue, have you addressed that issue, and you are trying to think of every single thing that could go wrong and be prepared for it. You can't just decide to go home because you won't be a good lawyer. We need to do the job right for our clients."

On Reputations

By Kevin Johnson (partner), Thompson Sizemore Gonzalez & Hearing, Tampa FL

"As a young lawyer, I remember attending a federal court hearing, watching a lawyer argue that his client should be reinstated, put back to work, and an injunction granted to put him back in his former position.

The judge, a very imposing figure, stopped the lawyer about 15 minutes into his argument. He says, *'Mr. Jones, have you read McKinnley vs Pate'.* The lawyer says, *'Well, Judge, I think I read that in preparation, but I cannot put my hands on it right now'.* The Judge says, *'Mr. Jones, I think you need to read McKinnley vs Pate, because in that case it was held that there's no such thing as substantive due process in the employment context.'* Now, how would you like to do that in front of a federal judge? My partner turned to me and said, *'And that is how you destroy your reputation in 15 minutes or less.'*

If you think about going in, arguing with the judge, and then making the judge go through that hearing—all on something where you haven't even read the original document, and you haven't even gone back and found out that there's no such thing as substantive due process in the constitutional plain—that judge is going to remember that. And, that's going to circulate. All the law clerks are going to talk about, *'Man, did you hear what happened in court today'*? That circulates. That's the nightmare we all dread, and that's why we spend the extra time preparing. I think once you've had some things go wrong, you understand the fear and the terror of losing in front of the jury. A lot of what we do is sometimes driven by fear, particularly with partners who are afraid of losing clients, losing cases, losing their reputation. All of us would love to be motivated purely by positive stuff and not by fear, but, sometimes, you are going to work for partners who are driven very much that way.

On Partner Expectations
By Kevin Johnson (partner), Thompson Sizemore Gonzalez & Hearing,
   Tampa FL
When I sit down and do an orientation with new associates, I tell them there are four things I expect from them: accountability, discipline, communication, and commitment:

- To me, **accountability** is about taking ownership of a case, and acting as if you are the owner of that case, not just the associate working on it. When you're accountable, you're living the case in the same way as if it was your client or your own business on the line.
- When I talk about **discipline**, it means you have to be your own toughest critic; that even though something may be good enough to get by, it's not good enough for you. That's very, very critical. You have to be willing to drive yourself to be better because you're the one looking at your work 100 percent of the time. Other people will just see parts of your work; they may not see the whole picture. But you, in your heart of hearts, know whether you have put in the level of effort that is necessary to the A+ effort. You need to have that level of discipline and commitment to get things done. Discipline also means going the extra mile to do one last search before going home for the day.
- **Communication** is another important factor. I've got to know that if something goes wrong that you are not going to try to fix it, sweep it under the rug, or come up with some crazy scheme. You need to find a way to get in to my office—even on the busiest days—and say, *'Look, I know you're really busy but I need two minutes of your time. I think we have a big problem with the such-and-such case.'* It's your job to get in front of me

and deliver the bad news; you need to say, *'This is my fault, we should have seen this earlier, but here's what I want to do to try to fix it.'*"

- The final piece is **commitment**. That you are committed to a long-term future as a lawyer. [In our profession], there are lawyers out there who cut corners, and trying to get clients to the door or doing things that are improper solicitation. The committed lawyer takes the long view, and does the right thing.

IN THEIR OWN WORDS

Q: How can a new associate to add value to the firm?

"Become proficient in multiple areas so [the firm's] partners can go to you when a project arises in your area." —RICK (CLASS OF 2008)

"Get involved in the community. Creating a positive name for yourself reflects well on your firm, and meeting new people provides the opportunity to generate business. Although most firms do not expect new lawyers to bring in new business for a while, it will eventually be necessary [for you] to maintain value at a firm (large or small)." —LISA (CLASS OF 2008)

"Work efficiently, and be able to learn new things quickly." —NIKKI (CLASS OF 2009)

"[Demonstrate a] strong work ethic and maintain/develop relationships that may eventually lead to business opportunities." —KELLY (CLASS OF 2007)

"Do rigorous research, write well, and stay on top of the case schedule and deadlines. Get involved in all [the firm's] cases, and have an opinion about the legal issues." —SHELLY (CLASS OF 2007)

"Be efficient and careful about your work product. The more time [the firm's] lawyers have to spend training, revising, and re-doing your work, the less money the firm is going to collect because they can't bill clients for training time and do-overs." —AMY (CLASS OF 2006)

"[You] must be willing to put in additional hours to reach the billable goals of the firm. For example, for every eight hours of billable time, 10 hours of work may be required. Also, [you] should get as much practical experience as you can prior to coming to the firm so you won't have that deer-in-the-headlights look when asked to do unfamiliar tasks. The experience will let you hit the ground running with a base of practicable knowledge." —Troy (Class of 2010)

"A new associate should learn that there are some things a managing partner has to handle, but there are other things that the associate can offer to do for the partners. Essentially, be a problem-solver. Find problems and solve them, or try to help solve them. The problem with many associates is that they sit back and wait for work to come to them, and then they wait for the praise or rewards. This does not work. An associate needs to take charge of their situation, and find tasks that they can do to help out the firm. Attend trade meetings, go to a conference on behalf of the firm, make phone calls, do follow-up on administrative matters, do PR. If an associate makes themselves valuable to the partners, they are going to get the rewards, and they are going to have job security." —Joseph (Class of 2007)

"The biggest thing a young attorney can do to add value is to be a sound technical lawyer in their practice area. " —Andrew (Class of 2007)

CHAPTER 15

There's a First Time for Everything

Congratulations on landing the job. Now, as a new attorney, you're going to experience a series of unforgettable career "firsts". This chapter, based on personal interviews, offers a glimpse into a few of the "firsts" experienced by other new lawyers. In time, you'll have plenty of your own to share:

Your First Week

As you begin your first week, it will be exciting AND overwhelming. New people, new environment, new processes and procedures. You'll wonder if there are enough hours in the day to do what needs to be done. A new associate from Savannah, GA, offered this tip: *"Starting a new career [in law] is stressful, but it's important to have a personal life. If possible, don't bring your work home with you."* Another associate observed, *"Work [at the firm] can be time-consuming and intense, but if you neglect to take care of yourself by not getting sufficient sleep, not exercising, or eating poorly, it will show up in some form in your work."*

Your First Intimidating Encounters

As a new lawyer, the best way to overcome intimidating situations is to conduct thorough research, and expect that more seasoned lawyers may try to use your newer attorney status to their advantage. When it comes to opposing counsel, associate Kassie Doyle says, *"They are going to look me up on the Internet, see my picture, and conclude, 'Oh, she's young, she's new', and a lot of them will try to bulldoze me. But you've just got to dig in and stand your ground. If you know your case law, and you understand the case, you say to yourself , 'This is why I'm right, and this is why he is wrong.'"* Associate Brett Lieberman recalls being in state court against an attorney many years his senior, and the two of them were disagreeing about a fundamental area of law. *"The guy was flat-out wrong,"* says Lieberman. *"He kept telling me, 'Listen, I've been doing this for 30 years'. And I said to him, 'But just because you've been doing the same thing wrong for 30 years doesn't make it right.'"* The key is not necessarily the length of time in practice or how large your law firm is, but to be prepared and to maintain your position—respectfully—in the event someone tries to bully you.

Your First Mistakes

Everyone makes mistakes, but a true professional doesn't try to hide them… especially in the practice of law. Accept responsibility for the mistake by telling your boss so that he or she can determine the best way to correct the error. Given that there could be legal ramifications (not to mention a potential need to put the firm's malpractice carrier on notice), it is not likely something that you as a junior associate can rectify alone. When advising your assigning attorney of the mistake, offer suggested courses of action. For example, let's assume you neglected to make sure that a certain document was attached as part of a pleading. The fact that a secretary may have forgotten to attach the document is irrelevant. Your signature is on the pleading, and it was you who failed to check it before it was filed. In this case, you go to the attorney and explain that the pleading was filed without the attachment, and admit that you failed to check the final product. Then you say something like, *"It will not happen again because from now on I will carefully review all filings."* Then, ask if it would be appropriate to amend the pleading to incorporate the attachment, or if there is another more appropriate way to handle it. Mistakes happen. You correct it, you apologize, you commit to not repeating the mistake, and you move on.

Your First Mentors

Mentors are more experienced, or differently experienced, lawyers who share their skills and wisdom with a more junior attorney informally or through a structured program.

Smaller firms are less likely to utilize a structured mentoring program, so it may be up to you to informally enlist the assistance of a more experienced associate from whom you can seek advice or guidance, or check in with to be sure you are on the right track. Note: some local or specialty bar associations offer mentoring programs to support new attorneys, which may provide a good option for those in partner only firms. Camille Iurillo, a small firm partner in Florida, encourages law students and new attorneys to engage in peer-to-peer mentoring by connecting with their contemporaries within the legal community. You gain a mentor and foster a relationship, she says. You expand your knowledge base, and build your referral network so that if the mentor's firm has to turn down a case due to a conflict of interest or because it is outside of their practice area, they may refer the case to your firm because they have a trusted relationship with you. Associate Brett Lieberman achieved a peer-to-peer mentoring relationship by forming a young lawyers' bankruptcy bar group. Some mentoring relationships, whether it be with a more seasoned attorney or peer-to-peer, evolve from networking opportunities offered through CLE's or bar functions, or simply from just connecting with an attorney you admire and frequently observe in court.

Your First Communications with the Partner

As you begin to identify questions or legal issues, ask yourself whether they can only be addressed by the partner, or if someone else can clarify matters. If a partner's feedback is not immediately needed, make your list of questions and issues so you can ask all of them later. If the matter *does* require the partner's attention, don't just pop your head into their office and throw around a hypo like you would with a classmate. Show that you respect the partner's time by presenting a short summary of the situation, what your research reveals, and your thoughts about how to proceed. Once you have your answer, write it down back in your office so you never have to return to ask the same question. Remember, the partner's clock is ticking away in six-tenths of an hour in unbillable increments, and they usually have a dozen other people and issues clamoring for attention. You do not want to have to go back later with an, *"Oh, yeah, I forgot to ask"*, or *"Oops, I forgot to mention."*

Your First Assignments

When you receive those first assignments, you can expect the assigning partners will be rushed and may only offer bits of information that you need to assimilate quickly. Here's the process to follow:

- **Clarify the assignment.** You might say something like this: *"So, you are saying that you need me to assume the jurisdiction issue is settled, to research point A and B only, and then provide you with a draft motion to dismiss by X. Do I have it right?"* The process of repeating what you think you heard will help you focus, and may prevent a misunderstanding; this technique also helps the speaker clarify what he/she said or to provide supplemental information.
- **Understand the assignment's purpose.** Associate Brett Lieberman says that to understand the assignment's purpose you should ask yourself if the partner is looking for an internal memorandum so he can advise a client, or is he preparing a summary of a motion to dismiss or a motion for summary judgment? If the partner wants to get something to his client first, he is looking for something persuasive. If he's looking for a

motion for summary judgment, he wants both sides; he wants to know your argument, he wants to know their argument, and he wants your citations to be perfect because he wants to be able to go into work, apply your analysis, and paste it into his motion for summary judgment.

- Clarify the assignment's due date. It's helpful to get a sense of the assigning party's expectations by saying something like, *"How much time would you estimate it should take me?"* Or, depending upon the assignment, *"How many hours should I spend on this before I let you know what's out there?"*

Now that you have the parameters of the assignment, you are ready to begin. Partner Kevin Johnson recommends starting this way:

> *"Whatever [the assignment is], start with the original document, otherwise what you are dealing with is an assumption. And assumptions will kill you quicker than anything, because you go in assuming the case is about X, and it turns out it's about Y. Or you assume the contract is written this way, but this is the one contract that is written differently. So, you have to start with the original document. I can't tell you how many times we have taken [new] associates back to square one and said, 'OK. Get out your rule book. Open up to the rule. Tell me what the rule says', and they read it and say, 'Oh'. That is not a position you want to be in as a young attorney. So, ALWAYS read that original document before you go into the partner's office or begin your assignment."*

Next, always read the entire case. Do not be tempted to rely upon head-notes or only cut-and-paste sections out of context without understanding the full case decision. If you get stuck, or wonder whether you are totally off track, go back to the partner for clarification only. You don't want to approach the assigning attorney by saying, "I'm stuck and don't know what to do next." Instead, explain succinctly the issue you are researching, what you are encountering, the direction the cases seem to be going, and then ask whether you are missing some facts or whether there is something else that you should be looking at. The assigning attorney would rather spend a couple of minutes filling in any gaps, or help you re-focus, than having you spend entire days on a tangent.

Now that you've completed your research, and are pulling together your document, treat your "draft" document as a final product. It must be carefully crafted, proofed for spelling and/or grammatical errors, and polished so that it reflects well on your abilities while instilling confidence in your work.

Your First Hearings

Newer attorneys are quick to be assigned to attending certain types of hearings, sometimes referred to as *suicide hearings*.

"When you first start out," says associate Kassie Doyle, "You think to yourself, 'Oh, my first hearing is going to be great.' I get there early, I've read everything on the cases, I've got three copies of highlighted case law with me, and I have everything laid out in front of me on the table...and then I just get destroyed. The first time it happened, I didn't know what hit me. [The hearing] was over before it began, and I was stunned and just stood there. Suicide hearings can be brutal."

Associate Brett Lieberman recalls some of his first bankruptcy hearings:

"When I first got to the firm, I was sent to court for two reasons: either, we were going to win (a slam dunk; we would be unopposed), or there was absolutely no chance to win. In other words, a suicide hearing. I might say something like, *'Your Honor, this is an unopposed motion. We sent out adequate notice, and everybody agrees. It's a joint order.'* And the judge says, *'Motion approved.'* Or, says Lieberman, the hearing might go against you. *"You get in front of the judge,* and say, *'Your Honor, as reflected in the pending motion before you, there are 17 well-reasoned arguments why my client should prevail.*

'I understand,' the judge says. *'Motion denied.'*

'But Your Honor ...'

'Counsel, I totally understand everything you're trying to say. Motion denied. File your response within 20 days.'

'Your Honor, could we have 30 days?'

'No.'

'Thank you, Your Honor,' and then you walk out of the courtroom. Hearings are tough. You win a lot and you lose a lot."

When it comes to your first hearings, small firm partner Camille Iurillo offered this advice:

"Always know about the judge before you appear before them. To learn about a new judge or proceeding, go early and observe. Oftentimes bankruptcy judges, or some state court judges, will hold a whole group of similar hearings at the same time. If you've not been before the judge before, get there early to listen to their other arguments. Even if they're in chambers, some judge will invite you in, or encourage you to observe, so you can understand how the judge operates and rules.

And associate Joseph D. McAllister shares his perspective:

"The most important thing is this, always be prepared! I may not be the smartest attorney in the courtroom, or have the most experience, or have the most polished style, but I always commit to my clients that I swear I will be the most prepared. Make sure when you go into the courtroom, or into a negotiation, that you know everything there is to know about the case and the law. When two parties disagree about the law, and you have two qualified attorneys, usually the one who is most prepared will win."

Your First Year

Take a personal retreat for a weekend, a day—even an afternoon—and reflect on how far you've come in a short but hectic period of time. You will be surprised to realize just how much you've learned and experienced, how many new skills you acquired, the challenges and fears that you've overcome, the clients you have helped, the relationships you have fostered. You are no longer a "new" attorney and have moved into the ranks of "newer" attorney. Yes, there is still so much to learn and absorb over the next few years, but you have made it through the greatest learning curve and the most difficult period of time. Celebrate your achievements. Express your gratitude to those who helped you along the way, not only those at work, but also your family, friends and loved ones. Take this time to reflect on your personal and professional goals for the upcoming year and then develop your written plan for how you will meet those goals. How can you become a better lawyer? Identify what you want to learn, new skills you'd like to acquire and new ways to develop professionally. Consider new networking opportunities you'd like to explore, relationships you'd like to cultivate, and how would you like to add value to the firm. Be proud of your success and all that you have accomplished.

IN THEIR OWN WORDS

Q: What are some of the errors commonly made by new lawyers?

"[One common error is] is over-confidence. There is no way a first-year attorney will know everything about an area of law. So, be confident, but admit when you don't know the answer to something…particularly if you're talking to a judge or a client." —KATHRYN (CLASS OF 2010)

"I have found many new lawyers are too aggressive. They believe that advocating for a client requires stonewalling opposing counsel, and being difficult for

the sake of being difficult. Creating and maintaining good relationships with colleagues is just as important as achieving a good result for a client."
—Lisa (Class of 2008)

"[Common errors] include working too fast and making sloppy mistakes; not understanding office politics; and not capturing all of their billable time."
—Amy (Class of 2006)

"Many new attorneys sometimes feel the need to be heard in large groups; during firm retreats or other lawyer meetings. Be careful of offering opinions and advice (unless specifically asked). It can be dangerous if political or other views are given that contrast with others in the firm or group. At social events, remember the rules of decorum. In other words, never be the drunkest person in the room. "—Adam (Class of 2006)

"[A common error] is marking down your own time because you don't think something should have taken you as long as it did. Or taking a project in the wrong direction because you did not want to admit, or didn't realize, that you did not understand the scope [of the task]." —Kelly (Class of)

"Not asking enough questions, not checking in [with the partners], and not following-up." —Shelly (Class of)

"[Some of the common errors include] taking things too personally; or making disputes too personal; or not managing client expectations or setting boundaries; not monitoring the revenue they generate to make sure they are profitable; and not keeping their reputation and integrity as a top priority."
—Keith (Class of 2003)

SECTION IV
INTRODUCING THE CORE COMPETENCIES

CHAPTER 16

The Core Competency Model

A core competency is, by definition, "fundamental knowledge, ability, or expertise in a specific subject area or skill set." In the context of a law firm, core competencies are considered "the behaviors explicitly expected of associates in all practice areas…"

In the smaller firm, they include:

Competency in business
Competency in associate skills
Competency in lawyering skills
Competency in personal and professional development

In brief, these core competencies are nothing less than a set of expectations about your knowledge, capabilities, behavior, skills, and attributes. They represent a model that has been borrowed from the business and human resources sector, and is now in use by large law firms as a basis for such personnel decisions as hiring, retention, advancement, compensation, and partnership selection.

Why should you care? Why does it matter if the large firms choose to evaluate associates and new hires on the basis of core competencies?"

There are several reasons to care: first, the Core Competency Model is already making its way from Biglaw to midsized and small firms. And your awareness of the model not only will keep you ahead of the game, but help to develop your competencies in law school and beyond. More important, an understanding and acceptance of the model will provide a means *to distinguish you from the other potential job candidates and to shine within your law firm once hired.* Looking further out in your career, you may at some point wish to lateral into a larger firm, or join a government agency, that employs the core competencies model, and your mastery of these concepts will be a clear hiring benefit.

In the four chapters that follow, we'll isolate the traits and behaviors essential to the core competencies. For now, let's begin with the big picture so you can perceive the overall scheme.

CORE COMPETENCES VALUED BY SMALLER FIRMS

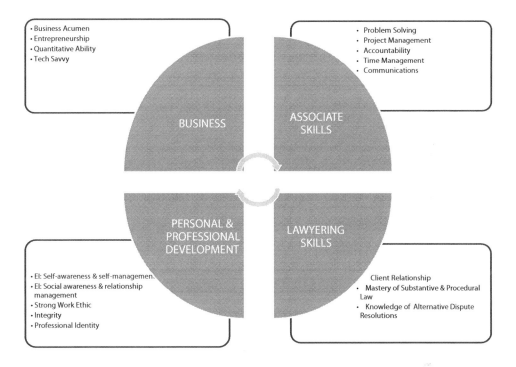

- Business Acumen
- Entrepreneurship
- Quantitative Ability
- Tech Savvy

- Problem Solving
- Project Management
- Accountability
- Time Management
- Communications

BUSINESS

ASSOCIATE SKILLS

PERSONAL & PROFESSIONAL DEVELOPMENT

LAWYERING SKILLS

- EI: Self-awareness & self-management
- EI: Social awareness & relationship management
- Strong Work Ethic
- Integrity
- Professional Identity

- Client Relationship
- Mastery of Substantive & Procedural Law
- Knowledge of Alternative Dispute Resolutions

CHAPTER 17

Competency in Business

The practice of law is a business, and if a law firm is to thrive it requires the application of fundamental business principles and skills. For this reason, business acumen—the knowledge and understanding of the financial, accounting, marketing, and operational functions of an organization—is the first of the core competencies under discussion.

Business acumen
Entrepreneurship
Quantitative abilities
Tech savvy

For most non-business majors (and this includes a substantial number of law students and young associates), a knowledge of business fundamentals is rough…even non-existent. And if you find yourself in this category, it's up to you to supplement your knowledge.

For those still in law school, it is recommended that you take such business-related courses as legal accounting, law office management, law and entrepreneurship, and marketing. For graduates, there are Continuing Legal Education (CLE) seminars, community college workshops, and webinars and podcasts for the basics. Many state bar associations have recognized this business shortcoming, and have created units within their organization to meet the need. For example, The Florida Bar's Law Office Management Assistance Service offers specifically created materials on such topics as Law Firm Financial Management for the Non-Financial Professional, Maintaining a TRUSTworthy Trust Account, Building the Small Firm Marketing Program, and Building Business in a Down Economy.

Other topics include:

- How to develop and execute a business plan and a budget;
- The basics of trust and escrow accounts;

- What you should know about cash flow, the billable hour, and client billing;
- How to collect on bills;
- Risk management;
- How to assess professional liability and the mechanics of malpractice insurance coverage;
- How to bring in new clients;
- How to network;
- And how to build the business.

To help fill in your gap in *business acumen*, seek out the Law Office Management Assistance Service (LOMAS) in your area. You'll find a list of LOMAS offices in Appendix C.

Once employed, new associates can build on their business acumen by remaining alert to information about existing clients, potential new clients, and relevant industry news. Watch for chances to develop new contacts, stay alert to potential speaking opportunities, participate in bar meetings, and network at conferences. Think about ways to get your firm's name out into the community by submitting an article for a state or local bar organization, or business journal. Any of these suggestions can demonstrate your understanding of the business of practicing law.

New Associates Need to Be Entrepreneurial

Entrepreneurs are *possibility* thinkers, and being entrepreneurial minded is an important competency within the business acumen cluster.

Jeff Cornwall, a business professor at Tennessee's Center for Entrepreneurship at Belmont University, defines entrepreneurship as *the process of identifying, evaluating, seizing an opportunity, and bringing together the resources necessary for success.* So, an entrepreneur is one who is open/alert to potential opportunities, and capitalizes on the chance to create or increase value. Entrepreneurs have a mind-set that sees the possibilities rather than the problems created by change; entrepreneurs are innovative and creative individuals who, as the saying goes, think outside the box as they explore, learn, and improve what is. Entrepreneurs also have a positive attitude when it comes to developing their business relationships; they are goal-oriented, and they thrive on incorporating innovation into their business endeavors.

It's easy to see how a business client would relish working with an attorney who takes an innovative, problem-solving approach. At the same time, new associates are cautioned to demonstrate their entrepreneurial competency with finesse. There is nothing less desirable to firm members than having a new lawyer tell them how to do their job. As a new associate, you need to learn the existing process and procedures while still cultivating the trust of your work group before making suggestions for change or improvement. At the right time, and under the right circumstances, your entrepreneurial competency will serve you and your firm well.

New Associates Need Quantitative Abilities

It's a given that capable lawyers need to possess a well-developed analytical ability in order to accurately assess situations and solve problems.

Law schools concentrate on developing qualitative case analysis skills with gathering and analyzing information. But little attention is given to the *quantitative* side of the equation, and that is a competency that can't be underestimated, especially for lawyers in smaller firms that lack specialists or departments to handle these tasks.

When it comes to *business acumen,* a solid quantitative knowledge will not only prove beneficial in the day-to-day operation of a law firm, but also when dealing with clients' affairs in cases ranging from calculating distributions and tax consequences in estate planning to financial documents for real estate transaction and business contracts and commercial applications, or for preparing financial affidavits with client assets in dissolution of marriage cases. The fact is, quantitative work is performed on a daily basis in the practice of law, and while it is often assumed that everyone possesses this competency, some new to the practice of law could benefit from a refresher course.

One's basic quantitative skills should include the following:

- The ability to understand business and basic accounting concepts and statistics, including those depicted in graphs, charts, spreadsheets, profit and loss statements, and tax returns.
- The new lawyer will also need to utilize basic math and financial concepts to calculating fees, damages, present value for structured settlements, proposed settlements, compound interest, interest rates, or for calculating profit margins.
- And…one's ability to apply mathematical reasoning, statistical methods, or a cost-benefit analysis to analyze and resolve business and technical problems, will be helpful.

Brushing up on your quantitative abilities will better prepare you to distill and analyze complex numbers in business or legal documents.

For those still in law school, this could involve taking a course in legal accounting or a course over at your business college or perhaps an adult education class. Basic reference books that can help fill in gaps include *Business Math for Dummies* (2008), *Reading Financial Reports for Dummies* (2009), and *Accounting for Dummies* (2008). For more specialized work, there is *Mathematics, Physics and Finance for Lawyers* (2011) and *Statistics for Lawyers* (2011). As stated, most law school graduates are relatively skilled at analytical and logical thinking as a means to problem-solving. We are taught how to gather, organize, and analyze information, conduct legal research, and use a logical, sequential and systematic process to formulate arguments or potential solutions. But to be an effective smaller firm lawyer, you must not neglect your quantitative skills development.

New Associates Need to Be Tech Savvy

Law firms need technologically savvy law clerks and newer associates because firms have limited time and resources to get these individuals fully productive. Firms seek new hires…

- Who are proficient users of word processing programs, basic presentation programs (Excel, PowerPoint), and web-based calendaring and docketing systems
- Who can quickly learn time and billing programs as well as case management and litigation support software.
- Who are efficient online legal researchers who are aware of free and inexpensive resources versus the full-service subscription services such as LexisNexis and Westlaw.
- Who are knowledgeable users of e-discovery and e-filing in both state and federal courts.

To be technologically savvy, learn about system encryption and data mining (a dicey new ethical problem for legal employers), and understand the applications of cloud computing. Develop an expertise so that you become the "go to" person for new technological resources and information. Follow blogs, subscribe to listservs or journals, and add the RSS feed to journals and other electronic media to your aggregator. These steps will keep you at the forefront of technological advances and the technology buzz. To further develop your skills in any of these areas, check out the ABA's Legal Technology Resource Center or your state bar for relevant webinars.

Four generations co-exist in the workplace today. It is not uncommon for members from each generation to have different experiences, values and expectations. Some even seasoned attorneys do not communicate via text message, and find it irritating to be with someone who is constantly looking down to check for text messages, or worse, who respond to messages while in meetings or in conversation. The same rub may be true for accepting personal phone calls during the business day. Quickly ascertain the expectations in your workplace environment regarding appropriate phone usage, listening to your iPod while you work, and communicating with others and respect them. To be tech savvy is also to be a competent and appropriate user of various communication mediums.

REFLECTIONS & GOALS

It's so easy to get swept away in the workaday world and overlook the vital step of planning for your professional development. Once you begin work, take time to develop your shorter and longer term goals (perhaps three months, six months, and one year to start) for increasing your business acumen. Sample goals could include:

- Set up Google alerts for news about your clients' businesses.
- Attend local bar mixers to meet other professionals.
- Participate in a service project within your community to expand your network.
- Make a commitment to have lunch with others outside the office at least once every other week.
- Submit information to your law school alumni affairs office for inclusion in the alumni magazine about your position and practice areas. It's a great way to generate referrals.
- Submit information to the state and local bar association publications announcing that you joined the X, Y, Z law firm that practices A, B, C areas of law.
- Stay in touch with classmates by sending periodic emails with updates.
- Draft and submit an article to a local newspaper or specialty bar publication.
- Find ways to help build awareness of your firm by making community connections. Example: if your firm practices elder law, volunteer to speak at a local senior center about living wills.
- Connect with your local public interest law organization to provide pro bono services to increase your skills (usually free training and malpractice coverage).
- Expand your network of lawyers and enjoy the reward of knowing that you have helped someone in need.
- Read non-law books on marketing, networking, people skills, and business. Example: *Outliers: The Story of Success* (Gladwell); *Blink: The Power of Thinking*

(Gladwell); *7 Habits of Highly Effective People* (Covey); *Never Eat Alone and Other Secrets to Success* (Ferrazzi); *One Relationship at a Time* (Ferrazzi); *How to Connect in Business in 90 Seconds or Less* (Boothman); *Difficult Conversations: How to Discuss What Matters Most* (Stone, Patton, and Heen).

CHAPTER 18

Competency in Associate Skills

Some years ago, an ABA Task Force charged with assessing legal education (the MacCrate Report) declared that problem-solving is one of the fundamental skills for new associates and law clerks. In fact, problem-solving is one of five underlying skill-sets in our discussion of core competencies that include:

Problem-solving
Project management
Accountability
Time management
Communications

New Lawyers Need to Be Problem-Solvers

The ABA Task Force report said problem-solving involved *the identification and diagnosis of a problem, generating alternative solutions and strategies, developing a plan of action, implementing the plan, and keeping the planning process open to new information and ideas.* Whether you're a new associate or law clerk, the goal of the problem-solver is to work through each of these steps before taking the situation to the partner. The last thing you want to do is dump another problem on their desk.

Another facet of problem-solving is to be a strong asset when a partner asks for feedback regarding a dilemma he/she is facing. Your ability to be open-minded and look at the situation from a creative, fresh approach with an eye toward the big picture can be very beneficial. If you recognize a potential situation, mention it to the individual who assigned the case, along with your suggestion for how you could bolster that argument, or perhaps research a line of cases on the issue to be best prepared. The attorney may agree and ask you to take the extra steps or they may determine that they are comfortable with the potential exposure or believe that the case doesn't warrant additional resources, but you have at least demonstrated a bigger picture perspective and that you are being proactive. This approach inspires confidence in your abilities.

Joseph D. McAllister, a third-year associate in Salt Lake City, shared his perspective on what it means to be a proactive problem-solver:

"If an associate makes himself valuable to the partners, he is going to have job security…and is going to get the rewards. Frankly, it does not matter what kind of problems you solve—legal, administrative, housekeeping, billing, computer technology, client relations, PR, etc. Just be a problem-solver. Find problems. And instead of complaining about them or avoiding them, solve them, or at least try to help solve them. Small firms don't have different departments to handle problems. You have one team and you work together…period."

Unfortunately, not all law students graduate with practical applications or a working knowledge of how to apply problem-solving skills. And while law clerks or new associates are usually adept at identifying a potential issue or problem, they are less skilled in providing a proposed plan of action to reach a solution.

It is a major competency gap.

Project Management

In the practice of law, attorneys coordinate large volumes of case files, data and documents, and distill these into manageable workloads for themselves and others. The planning, organizing, and team-building skills of a project manager are needed to orchestrate these tasks. To become an effective project manager, associates must develop their organizational ability, and be able to manage the flow of documents and information. While there are dozens of legal project management software products and systems in the marketplace, successful project management is a result of team-building and team management. A project manager or team leader must be able to motivate others even as members look to the team manager to resolve problems and issues that may develop.

Project management is an important element among the associate's core competencies. And here's a tip:

- Once you've been hired, you will want to have your office organized in such a way so that if the partner or team member walks in and asks you a question, you can readily put your hands on needed files or documents.

- If you have documents, schedules or, say, the court directory to which you constantly refer, create your own reference file or notebook so the information is always at hand (by the phone or your computer).

FOUR GENERATIONS IN THE WORKPLACE

It is helpful for the new attorney to appreciate that the advent of legal technology has had a huge and direct impact on various aspects of law firm project management.

If your firm has been in existence for 20-plus years, it is still possible that in a closet somewhere you will come across small boxes with 3 x 5 index cards in what constituted the old "tickler" system of file management. It worked this way: each file or case had an index card, and the box was arranged by month and day. A card filed, say, for mid-April, might read, "Duncan case: answer due on May 1". When the attorney or legal assistant checked on the day's activities, the "tickler" system would alert them to draft and file an answer before May 1st. Once completed, the card—with a new dated task—was moved further back in the box. There are four generations in the workplace today, each with different experiences, perspectives, values and expectations. Indeed, there are many, many attorneys and legal support staff still practicing and working in smaller firms who used that same tickler system…and a typewriter.

We share this information with you for two reasons: it underscores the dramatic technological changes that occurred in the practice of law in a relatively short period of time…AND the challenges for lawyers who came up through the 70s and 80s. Today, there are dozens of legal project management software products and systems in the marketplace to coordinate all aspects of project management: from calendaring, contact management, and tracking projects, to document management and assembly, performing conflicts checks, compiling time and billing. Indeed, many CLE's focus on legal technology, the bar journals are full of articles evaluating software, and every state bar conference features vendors demonstrating their products.

These rapid technological changes represent an extraordinary opportunity for most law students and new attorneys, for whom technology is second-nature. And your ability and willingness to help the firm evaluate new project management products, and assist others in the office to adapt to new systems, will be welcomed.

Accountability

Accountability means taking an active role and handling the assignment even when you've only been assigned a small piece of a bigger case. It is about accepting accountability for one's work, staying accountable for the progress made on the assignment or case, and providing updates.

> Associates who are accountable for their work—who take ownership of it—are also expressing a core competency. Here are a few tips:

- Even when you only have been assigned a piece of a bigger case, own it. Take an active role and handle the assignment as if it was fully your responsibility, short of actually acting without authorization.
- Anticipate the next step in the process, and ask about it to test your understanding and demonstrate your interest.
- Can you spot any red flags or issues that you may need to alert the assigning partner to or suggest an effective motion?
- If this was your case, what would your next step be? Offer to do the next step such as actually drafting the motion or writing the client memo now that it has been researched. Remember, you were hired to take work off a busy partner's overflowing plate.

Similar to "owning your work", accepting accountability for your work is about making and keeping agreements about behaviors, results and consequences. You are accountable for the progress made on the assignment or case. So, provide updates; if there is no formal mechanism for doing so, ask how the person making your assignments would like to be kept informed of the case status. For example, would they like a bi-weekly email summary? Even if formal updates are not desired, it's helpful to track this information for year-end evaluations (and possible bonuses) as well as your own professional development.

Accountability also means not dumping the problem on the assigning attorney, and expecting them to fix it. If you hit an impasse on an assignment or file, bring it to the attention of the assigning attorney…with potential solutions. Accepting ownership and accountability means an associate is willing to say, *"Look, this is my fault, I should have seen this earlier, but here's the way I suggest we fix it."* A law firm wants associates willing and able to accept ownership and to be fully accountable for all of their assignments and files. Mastering this core competency will help the firm transfer more responsibility to you, and for you to become a more highly valued member of the team. Kevin Johnson, partner in a 15-attorney employment law firm in Tampa FL, puts it this way: *"Accountability is about taking ownership of the case, not just [being] the associate working an assignment. Accountability [is a matter of] living the case as if it was your own client on the line or your own business on the line."*

Time Management

Everyone gets 24 hours a day, 168 hours a week, and 8,760 hours a year in which to work, sleep, commute, eat, exercise, recreate, and spend time with family and friends. The question is, how does the new lawyer choose to allocate those hours?

> One of an associate's core competencies is effective time management. Fortunately, it is a learned skill, but does require effort and self-discipline until the behavior is internalized. Here are some useful tips:

- Even if, as a law student, you enjoyed the thrill of pulling an "all-nighter"—cranking out projects at the last minute—this may conflict with others in the office, and could be perceived as a weakness. Attorneys have little control over external events, and if the new associate chooses to work down to the wire, he or she will be sorely challenged if they are suddenly required to cover an emergency hearing, or attend to a new client who has some immediate needs.

- Effective time management requires that lawyers give themselves sufficient time to complete the work product, and return to it a day later so it can be proofed with fresh eyes to make additions or catch potential mistakes. New associates must be prepared to do what it takes to produce quality work…even if it requires working into the night or do research at home or over the weekend.

- Punctuality is a subset of effective time management, and demonstrates that the associate respects their time and the time of others. At law firms large and small, punctuality is noticed and appreciated, even if it passes without comment. It applies to hearings, appointments, meetings…and assignments. Associates should submit everything (including timesheets) on time, and be sure assignments are not late. If it appears that the associate cannot produce a document on time, they must alert the partner. The partner may be able to identify a missing element, or change the approach, or extend more time, or decide if the associate needs help if time is of the essence. If the associate is concerned about the amount of time being spent on a project, the associate must check in with the person who made the assignment.

- To offer justifications (excuses) when you fail to meet a deadline creates a problem for the person who assigned the project, and provides them with far fewer options available at that point. Your job is NOT to create more problems for the already overloaded partner. Be conscientious about meeting your commitments carefully, thoroughly and professionally.

TIME MANAGEMENT TIPS

- Start your day off with the most difficult or least desired task so you get it out of the way while you're still fresh.
- Set aside time in your day to concentrate on high priority items or activities.
- There is always enough time for the important things. Throughout the day, continue to look for ways to free up your time for the important things.
- Use your smartphone or desktop calendar function to scan the month ahead so you can anticipate upcoming deadline and events and allocate time to accomplish what needs to be done.
- Before you leave the office for the day, take five minutes to plan for tomorrow so you can come in fresh with your priorities and tasks outlined.

Communications

Oral communications. According to malpractice carriers and bar disciplinary committees, the #1 complaint or grievance stems from an attorney's lack of communication. Yes, we know you can text and talk simultaneously… but how effective are your communication skills? One of the elements of a Competency in Associate Skills is your ability to listen carefully. It's called active listening.

TUTORIAL #1: ACTIVE LISTENING

Whether you are meeting with a client, interacting with the partner when receiving an assignment, or are appearing before a judge, you need to be able to demonstrate that you are listening carefully for several reasons. First, active listening improves mutual understanding. This developed skill will put the speaker at ease and show them that you care about what they are saying. It is a sign of respect that demonstrates that you value them. If you do not really understand what it is that they are concerned about, ask how can you do your best to help them? Second, it can be helpful to actively "hear" the speaker to determine what is not being communicated, or is being left out, to gauge what is needed for follow-up dialogue.

How do you actively listen?

- Allow no distractions.
- Do not be thinking about what you need to say next or something else you have to do later that day.
- Listen intently to the speaker.
- Maintain eye contact.

- Be empathetic. Nod your head in agreement as they speak to acknowledge what they are saying.
- Stay focused. Be attentive to what is being said.
- Use word prompts that encourage the speaker to continue such as ,"really" or ,"go on" or ,"I understand".
- Use reflective statements to validate. As in, *"I'm hearing that this has been an extremely frustrating process for you, Ms. Smith, but the reason we needed you to find all of the paperwork and bring it to us is because we will be required to file copies with the court to try to get the money that is owed to you."* Your simple statement validated the clients feeling and gave you an opportunity to help explain the process to them. Other reflective statements might include, "how so?" or, "you're saying …", followed by your paraphrase. Another way to use reflective statements is to be sure that you have heard someone correctly. As in, *"So you are saying that you intend to leave all of your estate to your dog, Max, but provide nothing to your daughter, Maxine, is that correct"?* This simple process of using reflective statements to let the speaker know that you are giving them your full attention helps both parties gain information while engendering confidence in you.

Public Speaking

A skilled lawyer must also be able to verbally present ideas in an organized manner, crisply, clearly and concisely. Honing these skills is an ongoing process that for many, began in law school, but needs to continue. Your ability to think on your feet and to speak with confidence comes with practice, practice…practice. Seek out "comfortable" speaking opportunities where you can continue to master this skill. Speak at a local school as part of your local bar's Law Week. Volunteer to explain health care surrogacy forms to a senior citizens group at their next lunch. Join your local chapter of Toastmasters. Speak clearly, deliberately (no ums or likes). Use proper pronunciation, and if you are unsure don't use the word. *The Articulate Attorney: Public Speaking for Corporate Lawyers* (Johnson, Hunter) is an outstanding resource for everything from overcoming nervousness, to engaging your audience, what to do with your hands, how to use inflection and pauses for emphasis, and much more. In the section on thinking on your feet, the authors recommend that you take "conscious control of the silence" before you begin to speak. When you first stand, don't say anything, just pause silently and use that time to think about what you are going to say rather than responding to the adrenalin rush with a staccato of words. In other words, don't rush to fill in a pause.

In a way, voicemail is also a form of public speaking. And communicating with a brief, clear, succinct message conveys that you are organized and well-prepared. Start with your name, provide a brief reason for the call, next your phone number stated clearly and slowly, and then repeat your name and phone number so the recipient does not need to listen to the message repeatedly.

Written Communications

An effective lawyer must be able to create a well-drafted document accurately, free of grammar, spelling, and word context errors, with no typos. It's a core competency. This representation of you and your communications abilities goes to the core of your reputation and credibility. You may present superb arguments, but you sabotage your efforts if the document is error-filled and gives the appearance that you are sloppy at best, or, worse, unschooled. Furthermore, proper citations are expected, just as your ability to use the appropriate format for a particular type of written document.

A well-drafted document is a core competency. Some suggestions:
- When you receive the assignment, be sure to ask whether what is required is a formal draft document or just a quick email outlining some issue. Then, think about the type of document that you are producing, whether it's a memo, a letter, a motion, or a draft, so you can either stick to the facts, produce arguments, or use persuasive writing when appropriate.
- If you are unsure of the appropriate format, find a similar work product that has been prepared previously (perhaps there is a form file on the firm's network server, or in the file cabinet). Check with a legal assistant or another associate to learn of a similar case).
- After you draft the document, check it carefully for mechanical errors and conceptual flaws.
- Be mindful of the audience or intended reader of the document. All written communication to clients should maintain a certain degree of formality, especially as a new attorney. And be sure you know your firm's policy on junior attorney's sending letters or emails to clients. For example, must the partners always read and approve materials before they are sent? Are the partners always to be openly cc'd on the email or letter, or do they only get bcc'd. Carefully follow all law firm procedures regarding correspondence.
- In general, view all emails as a written work product. Based upon your past usage you may assume informality is acceptable when in fact, just the opposite is true. Your email should be professional to reflect well on you and your law firm. Clients, as well as colleagues and others in the

firm, all form opinions of you based upon the written word they receive from you and you do not want them to mistakenly assume you lack experience or training. Be complete without abbreviations and use the same format (greeting, closing) as is used in a business letter.

TUTORIAL #2: EIGHT WAYS TO KEEP YOUR REPUTATION

With email, you create a permanent record that can be obtained and used against you (even once deleted). So, think twice about the content of your message, and whether a phone call might be more appropriate and effective. Ask yourself whether the information is sensitive or could be misconstrued or taken out of context. Also, learn whether there are lawyers or staff who detest receiving email (or worse, text messages), and for whom face-time is preferred.

Here are 7 more ways to keep your reputation intact:

Get to the point. Use the opening sentence of your email for your conclusion or request, and then provide your support or reasoning. It helps draw the reader into your analysis. If you provide four paragraphs of justification before your request, your direction is less clear, and the reader may overlook the true purpose of the message.

E-mailing or reply all? Know your law office's policy on this issue. In most cases, the "reply all" option would be a rare exception. It's easier to re-send your message to additional staff at the request of your boss, or for the boss to forward it to those she/he believes should have the information. Sharing email indiscriminately could be perceived as lacking in judgment.

CC or BCC? Know the office policy on this issue. In some firms, it is standard for an associate to BCC a particular legal assistant when the attorney sends an email about a client or case. Other firms may want you to copy the partner with whom you're working on a certain case. When in doubt, omit the CC; you can always forward the message later if it is determined the partner should have the information.

Forwarding messages. This is analogous to "email all", and is one of the quickest ways to impair your credibility. The act of forwarding someone else's message could create a level of distrust that would be hard to overcome. Others might worry that their messages will be inappropriately shared as well. If you do need to forward a message, go back and carefully re-read the entire thread to make sure that the information discussed at the beginning is relevant (and not improper) for the recipient to read.

Listservs. Make it a habit to check the sender's name to see whether you are responding to one person (as you may have intended), or responding to the entire list. Also, be judicious when responding to the list so as to not clutter everyone's inbox with a series of *"I agree's".* If you wish to poll the list on a particular topic, ask the members to respond to you privately so you can collect the responses from the individuals and then provide the compilation to the group. Your listmates will appreciate your resourcefulness by not receiving dozens of "yes" or "no" messages on your topic.

Attachments. Don't forget to include the attachment, and consider whether to convert the document to a PDF to prevent alteration.

Emotionally-charged messages. Never hit "send" in the heat of the moment, and never send an email you would not want seen on the front page of the newspaper. The potential of getting "outed" online is always present. We are probably all familiar with one particular email exchange between a legal employer and a disgruntled law student that was the subject of online humor that went viral. It could be worse. You might send an emotionally-charged email that is attached to a motion that is going to be heard by the judge. Still angry? Step away from the computer, cool down, and rework your message into an appropriately professional answer.

Non-verbal Communications

The most important thing in communication is hearing what isn't said," according to Peter Drucker, an influential author on management. When non-verbal messages are inconsistent with the spoken word, it results in ambiguity and confusion…and can be construed as disrespectful or rude. For example, you're sending the wrong message if you're tapping your fingers on the desk while listening to the firm's partner.

Effective lawyers are aware of the non-verbal communications of others. Imagine a situation where a client is smiling as they tell you they do not like you or the work you've done, or the expert witness who has a habit of chewing their lip and biting their fingernails. The non-verbal communications of both the client and the expert witness suggest they might not be credible. Or imagine this scenario: you're telling the firm's partner the results of your research on a legal issue. After a few minutes, the partner is involuntarily clenching her hands and tapping her foot. If you're a good observer, you process this unspoken message—*the message that isn't said*—and bring your report to a quick conclusion.

Of course, non-verbal communications is a two-way street. What do your non-verbal messages reveal about you? How about when the partner is regaling you with their courtroom prowess as you smile but tap your fingers in boredom. You may be thinking about the stack of work on your desk, but your non-verbal behavior could be construed as disrespectful or rude. Non-verbal communication—tapping your fingers, cracking your knuckles, playing with your hair, rolling your eyes, sighing deeply, crossing your arms against your chest—these all give away information you may not want to convey.

Feedback (the communications loop)

Formal evaluation programs are common in large law firms, and performance evaluations are the norm in law school. Small firms, however, are less likely to have formal evaluation programs. And in the absence of feedback, associates may need to ask for it...and prepare themselves that regardless of how good of a job they think they are doing, their employer will have suggestions about how to take the work to the next level. Can you accept feedback calmly and thoughtfully, without interruption or argument? The ability to receive—and grow from—constructive feedback is another in the bundle of communications competencies.

TUTORIAL #3: MAKING THE MOST OF FEEDBACK

Regardless how good of a job you think you may be doing, it's likely your employer will have suggestions about how you can take your work to the next level. Here are some suggestions about how to make the most of the employer's feedback:

- When receiving feedback, listen carefully and thoughtfully, maintaining eye contact with the speaker.

- Welcome constructive feedback. It will provide information you need to improve your performance.

- Do not interrupt and do not argue. Stay calm, detached.

- Don't take feedback personally. You cannot expect to know everything when you're just starting out.

- When the speaker has finished, thank them for being candid, and assure them that you will work on the issue or suggestion, or say that they have given you "something to think about".

- If you are comfortable and the circumstances seem appropriate, you could ask questions or request further clarification. Saying, "I'm not sure I understand," will encourage the speaker to elaborate. Or, depending upon the situation, ask how they would handle it, or if they could suggest more effective ways you might have handled the situation. Your goal should be to learn, incorporate the suggestion, adapt, and move on.

- If the feedback is unexpected, or is more information than you can deal with without getting emotional or being unprofessional, thank the speaker for the feedback, and say you'd like some time to think about what they said. Then, give yourself some time to process the information. Make notes about what was said, write down your thoughts, and then objectively evaluate the feedback. Think about it from their perspective.

- If the feedback is unsolicited, ask yourself if there was a triggering event or something that occurred that just brought the issue to the forefront? Perhaps you have a blindspot, or it is just something of which you were unaware, or it is a difference of perspectives.

- Remember that it is just as difficult to provide constructive feedback as it is just as it is receive it. Try to use the exchange as motivation to accept responsibility and see it as a learning opportunity.

CHAPTER 19

Competency in Lawyering Skills

For most small firms, the single largest source of new business is referrals from former clients and business associates. Cultivating client service and developing your lawyering skills is not only *the lifeblood of the practice of law*, it will be a key component of your success, and is the third in our series of core competencies. The elements include:

Understanding the client relationship
Mastery of substantive & procedural law
Having knowledge of alternative dispute resolutions

The Client-Savvy Attorney

As a new associate, your *first* client is the person who hired you, along with the other attorneys for whom you work. You must approach all assignments from a client-centered perspective, and put forth your best effort. It is only after you meet the needs and expectations of your internal "clients" that you can hope to interact with the paying clients.

After an initial new client meeting, law firms send an *engagement letter* that defines the scope of the representation, the services to be provided, the projected time involved in the process, and the expected fees and costs. When you receive a copy of the client's file, or are preparing to meet the client, be sure you're familiar with this commitment letter. It is the starting point for the relationship with the firm and the attorney assigned to the case. Also, be aware of any change in the representation. For example, if there was a need to go beyond the original scope of the agreement, you need to be familiar with the supplemental letter that modifies the terms and conditions. When the time comes to interact with the client, establish an appropriate counseling relationship that respects the boundaries of the lawyers' role.

Here are nine qualities of the client-savvy attorney:

- If the client is older than you, don't present yourself too informally or call the client by their first name unless invited to do so.
- Be approachable and down-to-earth without acting aloof or condescending. Listen carefully to what the client has to say so you can identify what is really bothering them. In the words of author Stephen Covey, *seek first to understand and then to be understood.*
- Put yourself in the client's shoes. They may be unfamiliar with legal jargon or concepts, and are uncomfortable, apprehensive, and insecure. Acknowledge their feelings to reassure them.
- Treat each client and their case like it is YOUR personal client, and become vested in their success rather than just completing an assignment. Your effectiveness will be compromised if you rush to file a lawsuit when all they want is an apology and an opportunity to be heard.
- At the conclusion of an in-person meeting, summarize what you will do for the client, what they need to do, and when and how you will next be in contact. Do not make promises you cannot deliver, and always deliver what you promise. Managing client expectations is a critical aspect of being a client-savvy lawyer. To avoid problems and potential grievances, be clear about what they can expect from you and what you expect from them. Partner Kevin Johnson puts it this way: *"Clients sometimes have unreasonable expectations. It's our job to control and shape those expectations."*
- Make sure the client understands that your role is limited to providing advice and guidance; that you will provide them with resources and the best information to see the options and outcomes of various paths… to help them to understand the time parameters involved…and to help them reason through a cost-benefit analysis. But they are the ultimate decision-maker.
- Consult with the client as appropriate, keeping them informed on what you are doing and what is happening (and return phone calls or emails promptly).
- You have an ethical obligation to tender all offers and implement any decisions made by the client. Document in a letter any items that you want to underscore, or when you have concerns about whether they really heard what you said. This step provides a clear record of requests that you made to them and information that you offered.
- Treat clients with respect, and recognize that when clients are satisfied with your representation, they will tell others. It's a cliché but true: a happy client will tell 10 people, but an unhappy client will tell 100 others.

Mastery of Substantive & Procedural Law

The first few years of practice are about building on your knowledge base, and your firm recognizes this is an evolving process. But even as you handle cases in subject areas that you know nothing about, you must be willing to do what it takes to learn new areas quickly and effectively. That was the experience of Kassandra Doyle, a second-year associate:

> *"When I walked in the door that first day, I did not know a thing about maritime law. Which was really strange because I'm very much a geek, and am usually over-prepared. So, I hit the ground running. I started bringing stuff home, reading books and articles, asking questions, and doing whatever I could to absorb all of this new information. It wasn't easy, but I kept going over it, and in time I became a lot more comfortable with maritime law. I was also very lucky because one of the benefits of a small firm is that it is like a family. I would get an assignment from a partner, and I would check in with my unofficial mentor, a senior associate, to be sure I was on the right track. I think the fact that I was willing to do all that really helped get me on my feet and gain an understanding of the law."*

As part of the mastery of substantive and procedural law, you must learn the law relevant to your firm's practice areas. For example …

- The relevant filing deadlines
- The legal holidays
- The statute of limitations for your practice areas and jurisdiction
- The rule on counting weekends as it affects computing time

And …

- Learn the litigation process for the trial and appellate levels in state or federal court for the type of cases your firm handles.
- Learn what administrative law regulations, agency rules, or procedures may apply to your practice areas.
- Whether your assignments or cases will be in state or federal court (and know that each court can have separate rules applicable to attorneys in that jurisdiction). Always check for special rules in each type of court such as bankruptcy, workers' compensation or family law, and for local rules in each geographic area. Be sure to consult the rules before filing documents. If the local rules impose a page limit or state that it will only accept documents electronically, or when accompanied with a yellow cover sheet, provide exactly what they mandate to save time and grief.

If you just need a quick perspective, don't overlook the value in secondary sources that you learned about in your first semester of law school, such as an ALR article about the topic or Am. Jur. or C.J.S. Depending upon the level of information you seek, CLE's are a great way to quickly absorb the law in a particular area. Fortunately, more and more inexpensive CLE's are now available as webinars. Are there bar sections specific to your practice area? Consult those sections' newsletters or journals for articles to expand your learning as you continue to develop your base of knowledge.

The Rules of Ethics and Professional Responsibility

The rules of ethics and professional responsibility, and the professionalism standards governing lawyers, is another area you must keep at the forefront of your mind...especially because a violation of these rules and standards can give rise to a grievance complaint, and bar or court-imposed disciplinary action against you. Also, remember that the rules of ethics and professional responsibility only set the minimum standards.

One ethical area that tends to snag newer attorneys is your duty of confidentiality. For example:

- Your obligation to maintain client confidences is paramount even if it may be tempting to discuss the case with your roommate, spouse, or best friend.
- Know the office policy about the removal of files from the office, and be vigilant so you don't compromise the case by leaving them in view.
- Never discuss another client's business with your client or they could justifiably assume you would share information about their case as well.

When dealing with issues of confidentiality, conflict of interest, or communication, there are so many situations (most recently, on social media sites or in blogs) where a new attorney can inadvertently run afoul of the rules. *When in doubt, ask before you act.*

Typically, you would begin by consulting others within your law firm. But there may be occasions when you should seek assistance outside the firm (for example, if you think someone in your firm has acted unethically, and you are concerned about your obligation to report them). With all that has happened in the mortgage and foreclosure industry, this is a situation that has occurred as some firms hired many new inexperienced attorneys to handle cases in a "mill-type" of situation. You could consider a call to your school's professional responsibility professor. Some young lawyers' divisions and local bar associations offer new lawyers' mentoring support programs, and almost all state bodies that govern lawyer conduct offer ethics hotlines to assist attorneys. Whichever avenue you choose to pursue, be sure to seek assistance so as to not commit malpractice or compromise your integrity. Again, the best policy is to receive clarification if you are unsure.

As regards professional responsibility, lawyers are expected to exhibit *professionalism*, a less clearly defined standard that demands a higher level of conduct such as practicing with civility and doing what is just and right. Displaying a lack of professionalism can also subject you to disciplinary action in a growing number of jurisdictions. Examples of unprofessional conduct that give rise to grievances include sending insulting and profane emails to opposing counsel; raising one's voice, yelling, or making disparaging comments such as calling opposing counsel or their client an "idiot" (or worse) during a deposition or hearing; engaging in conduct that was viewed as obstreperous or defiant.

Knowledge of ADR Options

As recently as the 1980s, the teaching of alternative dispute resolution techniques was not considered mainstream at traditional law schools. In recent years, though, ADR knowledge (mediation, arbitration) is considered one of the core competencies, and new lawyers need to be aware of the options in their area:

Mediation. As a quick refresher, mediation is a problem-solving strategy during which an impartial third person helps the parties (and their respective attorneys) craft a resolution to the issue. The attorney's role is to guide his or her client through the process, help the client re-focus if they get hung up on a particular issue, and help facilitate an agreement. Mediation is a dynamic exchange of information achieved with all parties respectfully and carefully listening to everyone. Mediation works best when the parties are ready and willing to settle their case. It is usually confidential, and the statements or settlement offers cannot be used in subsequent court or arbitration proceedings.

Arbitration. Arbitration proceeds more like a civil case, with the presentation of evidence and the examination of witnesses in front of a third-party arbitrator who rules on the case by issuing an award. The primary distinction between mediation and arbitration is who actually resolves the issue. In mediation, it is the parties to the conflict who reach a final decision that was facilitated by the mediator, while parties in arbitration present their sides to the arbitrator, who renders the determination. Negotiation is accomplished without a third-party intermediary between just the parties and their attorneys who work together to resolve the dispute.

Given today's overflowing court dockets and limited judicial resources, resolving conflict through alternative means without resorting to the traditional courts is prevalent. In fact, in many jurisdictions mediation is mandated for family law matters, small claims, medical malpractice claims, the foreclosure process, and workers' compensation cases. It also can be a contractually mandated dispute resolution mechanism between private parties. New lawyers need to know when mediation or arbitration is required in their jurisdiction and practice area, and that while an ADR option may not make the most money for the firm, it may be the right thing to do for your client.

Note: it is likely that the more seasoned lawyers in your firm lack formal training in mediation or negotiation. If you gain or have gained this skill-set, especially in a clinical or practice setting, your firm may relish having you handle these matters for them. If you develop a propensity for handling these cases, it may be beneficial to become a certified mediator, a step that enhance your credentials and makes you more valuable to the firm.

CHAPTER 20

Competency in Personal & Professional Development

When it comes to personal and professional development, the first core competency under consideration is Emotional Intelligence (EI).

EI is the ability to recognize and regulate emotions in ourselves and others, and it is divided into four major "domains" or categories: Self-Awareness, Self-Management, Social Awareness, and Relationship Management. You may be unfamiliar with EI, but the concept is clearly making its way into the law firm environment. And research shows that there may be a higher correlation between emotional intelligence and career success than between traditional intelligence (IQ) and job success. In fact, author Daniel Goleman (*Emotional Intelligence: Why it Can Matter More than IQ*), argues that a strong EI may account for up to 80 percent greater job success! In this chapter we will discuss the five core competencies in this category:

> **EI: Self-awareness & self-management,**
> **EI: Social awareness & relationship management**
> **Strong work ethic**
> **Integrity**
> **Professionalism**

EI: Self-Awareness & Self-Management

Self awareness and self-management—easily minimized and often overlooked—are integral to thriving in a law firm and being a productive attorney.

Think for a moment about how you are wired:

- Have you ever been told you are abrasive or unfeeling, or are you considered a caring and empathetic individual?
- Would your closest friend or partner characterize you as level-headed, or that you have problems managing your emotions?

- Would co-workers say you are sarcastic and a pessimist, or that you exhibit diplomacy and optimism?

The practice of law can put you in situations beyond your control, triggering anger in the best of us. So, ask yourself: are you prone to emotional outbursts? What if opposing counsel says something hostile or threatening in negotiations? Are you likely to blow up…respond in kind…fight fire with fire? If you recognize this trait in yourself, one of the core competencies is that you learn how to keep potentially disruptive emotions in balance by stepping back, taking a deep breath, and pausing before reacting.

Let's take another example: your reaction to stress.

Billable hours, demanding clients and supervisors, unpredictable outcomes; they can easily push one's buttons. Can you remain calm under fire? Does stress make you anxious to the point it immobilizes you, or are you able to recover quickly from setbacks? How might you react when the judge tells you in open court—in front of your client—that the case you were relying upon has been overturned? Can you keep small annoyances in perspective and not let them blow out of proportion?

Law firms do not view one's inability to handle stress as a positive trait; in fact, you're likely to be asked during your job interview about your particular stress management techniques. Self-knowledge is a powerful tool that can help us become a more satisfied and happier person, and a more effective lawyer. As you become more self-aware, you will be able to use this information to your advantage to "self–manage", by better regulating your impulses, your moods, and by exercising self-control. This is the essence of Emotional Intelligence (EI).

HOW WELL DO YOU KNOW YOURSELF?

Self-Awareness
- *Emotional self-awareness.* Being in touch with your own emotions and recognizing how they impact you. Trusting your gut feelings to guide you in decisions.
- *Accurate self-assessment.* Knowing your strengths and limits; having a "warts-and-all" understanding of what makes you tick. Being aware of your blind spots and to work around them.
- *Self-confidence.* Having a solid and realistic understanding of your self-worth and capabilities. Being comfortable expressing opposing points of views and making and executing tough decisions.

Self-management

- *Emotional self-control.* Keeping destructive emotions and impulses under control, and staying cool under pressure.
- *Transparency.* Displaying ethical behavior, honesty and high integrity; admitting mistakes, and being trustworthy with no hidden agendas.
- *Adaptability.* Demonstrating flexibility to changing situations or in overcoming obstacles.
- *Achievement.* Having a drive to improve performance and to meet inner standards of excellence.
- *Initiative.* Showing a readiness to act and seize opportunities; having an ability to self-motivate (being entrepreneurial and creative).
- *Optimism.* Demonstrating a positive, "can do" attitude.

EI: Social Awareness & Relationship Management

As mentioned earlier, self-knowledge is a powerful tool. It can help you become a more a more effective lawyer. How? Through social awareness and relationship management, which is the other half of the Emotional Intelligence equation. These two qualities will help you interact more effectively with clients and others in the firm, and help you find common ground and increase your empathy and understanding of others. For example, a competency in this area might help you perceive the underlying motives of which a client may be unaware. Is the plaintiff bringing suit for revenge? Is the defendant refusing to settle to punish the other side? Is the case less about receiving a large financial judgment and more about getting the client's job back?

Social awareness

- **Empathy.** The ability to sense and "read" others' emotions; understanding their perspective, and reacting sensitively and appropriately to their needs and concerns. Your ability to read people to assess the best way to present information can be highly beneficial in creating a positive work environment and in ensuring client satisfaction.
- **Organizational awareness.** Perceiving the undercurrents within the firm; recognizing the interplay of the power structure with social and political influences; understanding the practical realities; thinking in terms of the bigger, firm-wide picture.
- **Service.** A genuine interest in recognizing and responding to the needs and expectations of clients as well as others within the law firm.

The research on Emotional Intelligence suggests that one's competency strengthens with maturity and experience…and that it can be learned. If you feel less competent in some of the areas discussed here, be aware that with time, practice…and attention!…you can better develop this aspect of your intelligence. In his article on *Hiring Emotionally Intelligent Associates*, law firm consultant Larry Richard, JD/Ph.D., concludes by saying, "…*Emotional intelligence is not a peripheral, inconsequential irrelevancy, but rather a body of knowledge that gives you a roadmap about how to compete effectively with other well-run businesses that pay attention to the development of their human capital. If you hire associates who are smart and interpersonally effective, you will be on your way to building a world-class law firm.*"

Relationship management. Practicing law is about face-to-face inter-actions with staff, other attorneys, and clients. It is your ability to not only provide the technical answer, but to also be pleasant, understanding, and collegial, which will lead to your ultimate success. Successfully practicing law and *thriving* in a law office environment is predicated on three things: under-standing and managing ourselves, understanding and managing others, and understanding and managing relationships.

> Being brilliant and having "book-smarts" doesn't necessarily equate to pos-sessing people skills and being "people-smart." But balancing these "soft" skills allows you to be simultaneously people-smart and book-smart.

The following are core competencies in this area:

Inspirational leadership. Inspiring and motivating others with a com-pelling vision; leading by example.

Influence. This competency recognizes that different persuasive tactics are more effective in certain situations and with certain types of people. For example, empathy works best with some people. For them, you acknowledge that you understand their view and "where they are coming from", but ask them to look at it from a different perspective as you persuade them with your well-reasoned analysis. The art of influence is about knowing and evaluating different methods to determine the preferred method to present ideas in such a way as to influence or win people over.

Developing others. Bolstering others' abilities through feedback and guidance; mentoring.

Change catalyst. Initiating, managing, and leading in a new direction when needed.

Conflict management. When it comes to Emotional Intelligence, con-flict management is a critical competency. All too often, newer practitioners tend to avoid conflict so as to not "rock the boat." But when you learn to "manage" conflict, you open up new possibilities. The skill requires that you embrace potential disputes or disagreements, and work with the involved parties to resolve the conflict fairly and professionally for the good of all. Conflict management calls for an ability to defuse an emotional or stressful situation to get the parties to a point that options can be evaluated with a win-win in mind. This skill applies whether the parties involved are clients, other attorneys, office support staff, even a local bar committee.

Building bonds. Cultivating and maintaining a web of strategic relationships.

Teamwork and collaboration. Cooperation, consensus, shared commitment and team-building.

Strong Work Ethic

The third core competency within Personal and Professional Development is to cultivate and exhibit a strong work ethic. One aspect of a strong work ethic involves consistently creating a high-quality work product that is reliable, and does not require extensive proofing, editing, updating, or re-working.

Let's start with a draft document requested by the partner:

- **You treat a "draft" document for submission as a final product.** If you merely jot down a few ideas and present them (or worse, text them) to the partner, it won't build confidence or trust in your work. When a "draft" document is requested, it must be in the format appropriate for that type of document and error-free (i.e., spelling, grammar, syntax, word choice). This level of attention builds trust in the associate's work. The bottom line: *treat a draft document for submission as a final product.*
- **You return to the original document.** An often-overlooked aspect of creating a high-quality work product is to neglect the original document, whether it is a contract, complaint, letter, or case decision. You must carefully read and understand the facts contained within the original document before beginning to research all the applicable rules, statutes, and case law before formulating arguments. This step can minimize the waste of time by not pursuing false paths. Bottom line: *if you're unsure which is the best-reasoned approach, it may be helpful to outline an Option 1 and Option 2 so the partner can see the line of thinking and choose the best strategy.*
- **You make sure all your bases are covered.** A strong work ethic is evidenced when you're disciplined enough to chase down that last line of cases to be sure you have covered all of your bases, and that they are still good law. You do not want to be in the position of having a partner learn

from a judge (in open court) that your research overlooked a case or an overturned decision. The bottom line: *you will never be 100% comfortable with your work product because there simply are not enough hours in the day. But if you having a nagging concern about your research, double-check your work.*

- **You're well-prepared.** When a more senior attorney calls you into the office, your taking a pen and pad demonstrates that you're ready to work. Are you meeting with that attorney to discuss scheduling? Have your calendar accessible. The bottom line: *gather your thoughts before going into a meeting to be sure you have everything you need, are organized and well prepared.*

* **You anticipate the needs of others.** You will be a highly valued member of the team if you can anticipate the needs of others. If the partner notoriously neglects to bring the rules book to hearings, tuck a copy into your briefcase. If the partner is always short of quarters for the parking meter in front of the courthouse, keep a roll of quarters handy. The bottom line: *you want to be known as that person who is a team player, who anticipates the needs of others, and who is willing to go the extra mile.*

Integrity

Inspiring trust is the fourth competency in the category of personal and professional development. To a lawyer, reputation is *everything*.

With all the demands on an associate's time, it would be easy to downplay this vital concept, but it would be at your peril; in fact, there is no minimizing the importance of an associate's integrity and ability to inspire trust. And cultivating a solid reputation from Day 1 has an impact on the support an associate receives in the firm…what assignments they're given by partners… how they are perceived by opposing counsel and lawyers with whom they co-counsel…on the judges who decide their cases…and on their ability to bring in and service clients. As a lawyer, the new associate is an officer of the court, a serious obligation. And being known as someone who is responsible, of good character, and a person with integrity, is the hallmark of one's legal career and personal success.

An associate must (always) be truthful and ethical.

An associate shouldn't compromise their values or self-respect.

An associate shouldn't try to bluff their way through situations.

An associate is quick to recognize their limitations, and know when to seek guidance from others.

The new associate must also appreciate the fine line between being a zealous advocate and being known as someone who is willing to overstate or exaggerate facts or legal positions to advance a client's interests. Brett Lieberman, a third-year associate in a Florida law firm, shared this observation:

"... I've seen my senior partner go before judges who know him, and the things he says have more traction than if I was to say the exact same thing because he has developed a relationship of honesty, and of fairly and reasonably representing his clients. [On the other hand], I've seen other lawyers almost lie to judges. It seems like the most knowledgeable judges know every single thing, and if what you say in court is a misrepresentation, or if you are being disingenuous, the judge will remember. [Over time], you build a reputation, and you have to stand by it because your reputation is what precedes you."

Inspiring trust is just as important. Partner Kevin Johnson, an employment litigator, explains:

"Trust is integral to the successful practice of law. When we go out and get clients, we are trying to get them to trust our wisdom, our judgment, our knowledge. It's a trust relationship. We work very hard to sell our firm and ourselves as people who have the right answers, and who can be trusted with the client's personal life, their business life, and everything that they care about. And if we're going to introduce you—the new associate—into that trust relationship, we need to trust you as well. We need to believe that you are going to know which questions you should be answering and what questions you shouldn't, when you should call the client and when you shouldn't, and that if we send you out to get an answer, we can trust that what you bring back has been very, very thoroughly researched. And if we go with that answer, that we are not going to be embarrassed [in or out of court] when the correct answer turns out to be 180-degrees from what you brought us."

One final aspect of integrity is one's professional demeanor and appearance. A disheveled or sloppy look—even taking Casual Friday too far—can undermine the associate's efforts to be taken seriously. It may even call the associate's judgment into question. New associates must be impeccable in their grooming, hair style, and choice of clothing. All these are elements of one's overall professional demeanor. The associate never knows when they may be called upon to cover a hearing, meet with a client, or talk to someone who stops by the office. The associate also must be mindful that they are only as good as their reputation, and that word travels fast in the small and interconnected legal community. This applies even outside of work or after hours. A seemingly minor incident of unprofessional conduct can adversely impact one's credibility and reputation.

Professional Identity

Professionalism goes to who you are, how you treat others, and the image that you portray. Professionalism is also about going beyond the rules of ethics that provide the minimum standard of conduct. One aspect of professionalism, one's professional identity, is the fifth competency in the category of personal and professional development. As a new practitioner, you need to maintain your professionalism in person as well as online and in the media. Electronic professionalism, or "E-professionalism" as it is sometimes called, is concerned with how a person is depicted, and how they conduct themselves professionally, in the electronic world.

> Are you aware of your online persona? Think of it as your personal "brand". Does it present a reputable image for the firm and for you as a legal professional?

These days, as part of their due diligence, employers (and recruiters and HR professionals) are routinely checking prospective employees' social networking persona, and often basing hiring decisions on found information. In fact, recent surveys indicate up to 70 percent of those hiring are using online resources in their hiring process. An impulsive or angry blog post, or a goofy YouTube video, could have unforeseen consequences. The Internet is filled with stories of employees who were fired, or *"dooced,"* because of information, pictures, or blog posts. New associates need to think like an employer (or opposing counsel, or prospective client, or jurist), and review the information about themselves at Google, Yahoo, Facebook, LinkedIn, etc. Remember, deleted Internet sites and email messages can be retrieved and are "discoverable". Digital is forever; there is no such thing as an eraser on the Internet.

Once you're hired, be sure you know your firm's Internet policy, and make the most of your digital persona. Consider gaining some positive attention (and publicity for the firm) by submitting information that you volunteered to chair the holiday toy drive for your Young Lawyers Division of the Bar, or that you presented a workshop on understanding legal responsibilities for new adults to a group of high school seniors, or that you have joined the xyz firm to your state or local bar news. Most employers welcome this type of self-promotion (especially if you offer to also prepare a release about your partner's accomplishments).

APPENDIX

The Upside of Small Town Law

By Richard L. Hermann, Esq.

When I was a 3L, my law school dean called me into his office and told me that he had recommended me to a 65-year old alumnus who practiced in a small town in New York State's Southern Tier, and who was looking for a successor to mentor. The Dean said that I "fit the profile" because I grew up in a similar small Western New York town. Intrigued, my wife and I headed out to what we thought was the ends of the Earth to spend the day with the attorney and his wife and scope out the opportunity.

From Wall Street to Main Street

The country practitioner lived in a stunning home with a fantastic view, on top of a hill that overlooked the small community. He and his wife both drove very expensive cars and it was obvious from their surroundings that he was doing exceptionally well in his pastoral milieu.

It turned out that he did not exactly fit my preconceived notion of a rural practitioner. And the tale of how he arrived in rural America is worth telling for its instructional value:

> He had been an equity partner in a major Wall Street law firm until age 50 when, like so many people at the midlife point, he began to wonder if the grind was still worth it, and if what he had been doing so successfully was "all there is." He spent several months researching the legal market throughout New York State with the intention of identifying underserved communities. He eventually zeroed in on little Alfred, NY in Allegheny County, the second poorest county in the state. But, as his research revealed, the county's dismal economy camouflaged the relative prosperity of the village which, in addition to having no lawyers, was home to two academic institutions, one a university, the other a state college. Out of Alfred's population of under 3,500, there were a disproportionate number of reasonably well-paid professors and college

administrators. Within a year of relocating to Alfred, this very shrewd attorney was outside counsel to both academic institutions, had established a thriving general practice, and was in the process of building a high-rise apartment building to supplement a chronic dearth of on-campus student housing.

Despite a very attractive job offer, as well as an offer to pay my wife's law school tuition at a law school an hour distant, we graciously declined in favor of legal life in the big city.

That Was Then…This Is Now

Rural America isn't what it used to be. And that is mostly a good thing if you happen to be an attorney interested in a rural practice.

The transportation and telecommunications revolutions have homogenized our country to such an extent that the advantages and amenities—as well as some of the disadvantages—of metropolitan areas have crossed the divide and are seeping into less populated regions. Cable TV, the Internet, chain stores, good restaurants, multiplex cinemas, and the dispersion of high-culture entertainment even into remote locales (the small town where we have a second home has a huge concert shell that gets many of the same artists that appear in New York, Washington, Chicago and San Francisco, among them Willie Nelson, the Dave Matthews Band, and Yo Yo Ma). If you happen to be in a college town—and there are over 4,200 of those—you can find a great deal of good conversation and intellectual fodder to boot.

Taxes are often lower.

Crime rates do not come close to urban areas.

Living standards for professionals are quite high.

Work-life balance is virtually a given.

And guess what?

Rural America is still very much underserved by the legal community. Moreover, housing is affordable, commuting to and from work is a piece of cake, and schools have fewer problems than their urban counterparts, albeit drugs, sex and violence have also made their way into the youth population in rural areas. A recent survey of the top high schools in America included a solid representation of rural institutions.

The Beckoning of the Land

You are much more likely to see the inside of a courtroom much sooner in your career in the country than you will in the big city. You will also find that civility among opposing counsel still largely exists, if only because they see each other in court and across the negotiating table much more frequently, so there is a premium in acting mature, restrained and civil.

Another huge factor is the aging of the rural attorney population, a disproportionate number of whom are baby boomers on the cusp of retirement. Rural area practitioners are significantly older than their urban counterparts. Between 2011 and 2026, the retirement rolls will be overflowing with these lawyers.

Another attractive feature is the stability of a rural practice.

Change is slower, easier to accommodate, and much more predictable in a rustic setting. The population is nowhere near as transient as in metropolitan areas, and loyalty to service providers is paid a higher premium than in more urban settings. Rural areas also seem to spawn as much entrepreneurialism as you will find anywhere else. Small business startups are very common, and here again, complexity in launching and running a business in a federalist system requires considerable legal input. The increasing regulatory intrusiveness of government at all levels means an increasing demand for legal services.

While America's farm population has been suffering from attrition for 75 years, with no end in sight, farm families sit atop land whose values can exceed thousands of dollars an acre and whose mineral rights in this age of the drive for energy independence have enormous dollar potential. The natural gas industry in the gas-rich Appalachian region stretching from Central and Western New York down into Pennsylvania, Maryland and West Virginia anticipates drilling 70,000 wells in the next five years, and has increased its regional gas industry employment rolls by more than 50 percent.

Making the Move

Law practice sales ads are now a fixture on Web sites such as Craigslist, for example. Many of these are aging small-town lawyers concerned about identifying and luring a competent replacement. To a much greater extent than in major cities, these rural practitioners are much more willing to mentor their putative successors during an overlap period and to introduce them around town, thanks to a love of and loyalty to their close-knit community.

It is far easier today to undertake location research than it was back when the Wall Street lawyer performed his due diligence on possible rural practice locations in Upstate New York. Web sites like the Avery Index (www.averyindex.com) can tell you essential information like the per capita attorney population of each state. As this is being written, the big winners for the lowest numbers are:

State	Number of Attorneys Per 10,000 Residents
North Dakota	4.4
Arkansas	5.3
South Dakota	5.8
Kansas	5.8
Idaho	6.1
Iowa	6.2
Wisconsin	6.8
New Mexico	6.9
Indiana	6.9
Kentucky	7.1

These are extremely attractive statistics if you contemplate a rural relocation and practice. Especially when compared to the Big Legal Kahuna—the District of Columbia—with its 276.7 lawyers per 10,000 residents. In Washington, DC, you can throw a stick out of your office window and be certain that it will bounce off of at least five attorneys before it hits the pavement.

When you look at the Avery Index numbers, you need to be sufficiently sophisticated to note that the distribution of per capita attorneys is going to be highly uneven from one part of a state to another. What that means is that rural areas that are part of very heavily populated states may nevertheless be attractive practice locations. You can drive for hundreds of miles through parts of California, Texas, New York, Florida, Pennsylvania, Ohio, Illinois, Michigan, and New England that are so bereft of cities and masses of humanity that you think that you are in the Dakotas, Arkansas or Kansas.

The costs of entry into solo practice have plummeted everywhere, thanks to the technology revolution, and are even lower in rural areas. Computerized legal research options have relegated hard copy law libraries to the dustbin of history along with quill fountain pens and reading the law in lieu of attending law school. With competition to Westlaw and Lexis, legal research is becoming less expensive at the same time that it is becoming more expansive. Word processing software means that you really do not need a secretary, certainly not when you are in an initial launch phase of your practice. Voicemail can serve as a bargain basement receptionist. A home office is an easy thing to establish and can serve you ably until you begin to generate cash flow. Moreover, zoning restrictions are much looser in rural America.

Alternatively, if you feel that an office is essential from the outset, rent is generally cheap, far less expensive than in urban areas.

I know an attorney in a rural locale who rents 3,000 square feet of space above the local bank (a great location for referral business from the first floor) for—are you ready for this? - $125 per month! His landlord has not raised his rent in this century. In contrast, 3,000 square feet in downtown Washington, DC is now going for more than $12,000 per month with an annual 3.5 percent escalator and real estate tax pass-through! This attorney's offices are as nicely appointed as any partner's office in a large law firm.

Marketing your practice in a small community is also easier and cheaper.

Rotary, Kiwanis, Elks, Moose and Lions clubs abound, and are always eager for new members and for speakers on topical matters. Local newspapers are often keen for new arrivals to interview and may even accord you op-ed page space in print and online for a legal advice column. Local bar associations are excellent referral agencies. Becoming active in the community can also pay off handsomely. A rural attorney I know even went so far as to join five churches. On Sunday morning, he made the rounds of services and positioned himself outside the church entrances at the end of Sunday services in order to meet, greet and hand out business cards to fellow parishioners. While that is admittedly extreme promotional behavior, it is probably also unnecessary in most rural locations. In summary, there is a lot to recommend to attorneys seeking something different from the conventional career route. America is full of small ponds conducive to the arrival of big and small legal fish.

By Richard L. Hermann, Esq.
The New Lawyer's Survival Guide, Vol. 1: From Lemons to Lemonade in the New Legal Job Market (2012)

State Bar Associations & Small Firm Sections

Many states have specific small-firm related sections which can be extremely useful tools for schools that are looking to develop relationships with small firm attorneys. Generally, the purpose of these sections is:

> To provide a forum for the discussion of problems of common interest to small firm practitioners; To advance the quality of legal services provided by small firm practitioners; To provide a forum for the creation, discussion, advancement, and implementation of ideas to accomplish the foregoing purposes; To sponsor CLE programs for solo and small firm practitioners; and To provide a professional support network for solo and small firm practitioners.

Other state bar associations have Law Firm Practice Management sections that are designed to assist solo and small firm attorneys with practice management issues. Here, the emphasis is typically on practical programs addressing the nuts and bolts of small firm management. These sections are typically populated by small firm attorneys who are excellent resources for CSO staff.

General Practice Sections are another good resource for seeking out small firm attorneys. These sections are typically concerned with matters of interest to the general practitioner, including developments in legislation, regulation, practices and procedures in all areas of general practice and their impact on law office management.

It's also very important that you know the demographics of each relevant section. For example, the Arizona section is comprised mostly of solo attorneys, and not many small to mid-sized firms. Knowing that ahead of time can save a lot of time and effort in terms of outreach!

American Bar Association: General Practice Solo & Small Firm Division:
www.americanbar.org/groups/gpsolo.html

Alabama: Practice Management Assistance Program
(www.alabar.org/pmap/index.cfm)

Arkansas: Solo, Small Firm & Practice Management Section
(www.arkbar.com/Section/SectionInfo.aspx?id=9)

Arizona: Solo Practice/Small Firm Section
(www.azbar.org/sectionsandcommittees/sections/
solepractitionerandsmallfirm)

California: Solo and Small Firm Section (http://solo.calbar.ca.gov/)

Colorado: Solo Small Firm Practice Section
(www.cobar.org/index.cfm/ID/20156/SO/SM/Solo-Small-Firm-Practice/)

Connecticut: General Practice Section (www.ctbar.org/Sections%20
Committees/Sections/SmallFirmPracticeManagement.aspx)

Washington, D.C.: Law Practice Management Section
www.dcbar.org/for_lawyers/sections/join.cfm

Delaware: Small Firms and Solo Practitioners Section
(www.dsba.org/sections/small_firms.htm)

Florida: General Practice Solo and Small Firm Section
(www.floridabar.org/DIVCOM/PI/CertSect.nsf/Sections?OpenForm)

Georgia: Law Practice Management Program (www.gabar.org/programs/
law_practice_management/)

Hawaii: No specific small firm, practice management or general practice
sections (www.hsba.org/sections.aspx)

Idaho: Law Practice Management Section
(www2.state.id.us/isb/gen/sections.htm. Click on the Law Practice
Management Section)

Illinois: General Practice, Solo, and Small Firm Section
(www.isba.org/sections/generalpractice)

Indiana: General Practice, Solo and Small Firm Section
(www.inbar.org/ISBALinks/Sections/SectionsPublic/
GeneralPracticeSoloSmallFirm/tabid/271/Default.aspx)

Iowa: General Practice Section
(http://iabar.net/displaycommon.cfm?an=1&subarticlenbr=210
Click on the General Practice Section. Must be a member to access this
information).

Kansas: Solo and Small Firm Section
(www.ksbar.org/sections/solo/index.shtml)

Kentucky: Small Firm Practice & Management Section
(www.kybar.org/Default.aspx?tabid=372)

Louisiana: Solo and Small Firms Section (www.lsba.org/2007Solo/)

Maine: General Practice Section (www.mainebar.org/sections.asp)

Maryland: Solo and Small Firm Practice Section
  (www.msba.org/sec_comm/sections/solo/index.asp)

Massachusetts: General Practice, Solo & Small Firm Section (http://massbar.
  org/member-groups/sections/general-practice,-solo--small-firm)

Michigan: General Practice Section (www.michbar.org/general/),
  The Law Practice Management Section (www.michbar.org/lawpractice/)

Minnesota: General Practice, Solo & Small Firm Section
  (www2.mnbar.org/sections/general-practice/index.asp)

Mississippi: No specific small firm, practice management or general practice
  sections (www.msbar.org/section.php. A small firm listserv is available for
  Bar members only).

Missouri: Solo/small firm committee (http://lawyers.mobar.org/)

Montana: No specific small firm, practice management or general practice
  sections (www.montanabar.org/displaycommon.cfm?an=6#sections)

Nebraska: General Practice section (www.nebar.com/). Must be a state bar
  member to access Web site information.

Nevada: No specific small firm, practice management or general practice
  sections (www.nvbar.org/Sections/Sections.htm)

New Hampshire: No specific small firm, practice management or general
  practice sections (www.nhbar.org/about-the-bar/join-a-nh-bar-
  association-section.asp)

New Jersey: No specific small firm, practice management or general practice
  sections (www.njsba.com/committees_sections/)

New Mexico: Solo/Small Firm Section (www.nmbar.org/AboutSBNM/
  sections/SoloSmallFirm/solosmallsection.html)

New York: General Practice Section (www.nysba.org/
  "Sections / Committees" (on left) "General Practice Section)

North Carolina: General Practice Solo and Small Firm Section
  (http://gpsmallfirmandsolo.ncbar.org/)

North Dakota: No specific small firm, practice management or general
  practice sections. (www.sband.org/Sections/)

Ohio: Solo, Small Firms and General Practice section
  (www.ohiobar.org/pub/?articleid=115). Click on Committee and Section
  Chairs. The Web site is available to state bar members only.

Oklahoma: General Practice/Solo and Small Firm Section
  (www.okbar.org/members/sections/#general)

Oregon: Sole & Small Firm Practitioners (www.osbar.org/sections/ssfp.html)

Pennsylvania: Solo and Small Firm Practice
  (www.pabar.org/public/sections/genco/)

Rhode Island: No specific small firm, practice management or general practice sections
(www.ribar.com/For%20Attorneys/Bar%20Committees.aspx)

South Carolina: Solo and Small Firm Section
(www.scbar.org/Sections/SoloandSmallFirmSection.aspx)

South Dakota: Sole Practitioner and Small Office Section
(www.sdbar.org/memberspublic/Sections.shtm). Must be a member to access the information

Tennessee: General, Solo & Small Firm Practitioners
(www.tba.org/sections/GSSMLaw/)

Texas: General Practice, Solo and Small Firm Section (http://gpsolo.com/)

Utah: Solo, Small Firm & Rural Practice Section
(www.utahbar.org/sections/solo/Welcome.html)

Vermont: Small Practice Section Chair is John C. Thrasher Esq, Ceglowski & Thrasher LLC. Email: thrasher@c-tlaw.com
List of current section chairs may be found at:
www.vtbar.org/Upload%20Files/attachments/committees.pdf

Virginia: General Practice Section
(www.vsb.org/site/sections/generalpractice/)

Washington State: Solo and Small Practice Section (www.wsba-ssp.org/)

West Virginia: No specific Sole Practitioner and Solo Practice Firms Section
(www.wvbarassociation.org/divisions.asp)

Wisconsin: General Practice Section
(www.wisbar.org/AM/Template.cfm?Section=General_Practice_Section),
Law Office Management Section (www.wisbar.org/AM/Template.
cfm?Section=Law_Office_Management_Section)

Wyoming: No specific small firm, practice management or general practice sections.
(www.wyomingbar.org/resources/member_services.html#sections)

APPENDIX C

State Bar Practice Management Sections

The practice management or law office management section of your state bar association often provide a wealth of information about the business of practicing law. They offer online resources, forms, information and programs all designed to help the smaller firm practitioner learn about topics from trust accounts, to maintaining confidentiality of records, to record retention policies to project management software resources and much more.

Alabama
Law Office Management Assistance
    Program
Alabama State Bar
415 Dexter Avenue
Montgomery AL 36101
(334) 269-1515

Arizona
Law Office Management Assistance
    Program
State Bar of Arizona
4201 N. 24th Street, Suite 200
Phoenix, AZ 85016-6288
(602) 340-7355, www.myazbar.org

Colorado
Colorado Bar Association
Suite 950
1900 Grant Street
Denver CO 80203-4336
(303) 824-5320, www.cobar.org

District of Columbia
The District of Columbia Bar
1250 H Street, NW, 6th Floor
Washington, D.C. 20005
(202) 737-4700

Florida
Law Office Management Assistance
    Service
The Florida Bar
651 E. Jefferson Street
Tallahassee FL 32399-2300
(800) 342-8060 ext 5611, 5795 or 5794

Georgia
Law Practice Management Program
State Bar of Georgia
104 Marietta Street, NW, Suite #100
Atlanta, GA 30303
(404) 527-8770, www.gabar.org

Louisiana
Law Office Management Assistance
 Program
Louisiana State Bar Association
601 St. Charles Ave.
New Orleans, LA 70130
(504)619-0153

Maryland
Law Office Management
Maryland State Bar Association
520 West Fayette Street
Baltimore, MD 21201
Telephone: (410) 685-7878, www.msba.org

Massachusetts
Law Office Management Assistance
 Program
31 Milk Street, Suite 810
Boston, MA 02109
(857) 383-3250, www.masslomap.org

Michigan
Practice Management Advisor
Practice Management Resource Center
State Bar of Michigan
306 Townsend Street
Lansing, MI 48933-2083
(517) 346-6381, www.michbar.org

Missouri
Missouri Bar
326 Monroe Street
P.O. Box 119
Jefferson City, MO 65102-0119
(573) 635-4128

New Hampshire
New Hampshire Bar Association
Phone: (603) 224-6942

New York
Law Practice Management Department
New York State Bar Association
One Elk Street
Albany, NY 12207
518-487-5595

North Carolina
Center for Practice Management
North Carolina Bar Association
PO Box 3688
Cary, NC 27519
(919) 657-1580, www.ncbar.org

Oklahoma
Management Assistance Program
Oklahoma Bar Association
P.O. Box 53036
Oklahoma City, OK 73152
(405) 416-7051

Oregon
Personal and Practice Management
 Assistance
Oregon State Bar Professional Liability
 Fund
P.O. Box 231600
Tigard, OR 97281-1600
(503) 684-7425

Pennsylvania
Law Practice Management
Pennsylvania Bar Association
313 Bridal Path Rd.
Lansdale, PA 19446-1565
(215) 628-9422

South Carolina
Practice Management Advisor
South Carolina Bar
P.O. Box 608
950 Taylor St.
Columbia, SC 29202
(803) 799-6653, www.scbar.org/pmap

Washington State
Law Office Management Assistance
    Program
1325 Fourth Avenue, Suite 600
Seattle, WA 98101-2539
(206) 727-8237

Wisconsin
Law Office Management Assistance
    Program
State Bar of Wisconsin
5302 Eastpark Blvd.
P.O. Box 7158
Madison, WI 53707-7158
(608) 250.6012

Vermont
Law Practice Management Program
Vermont Bar Association
35-37 Court St.
P.O. Box 100
Montpelier VT 05602
(802) 223-2020

APPENDIX D

Recommended Books, Web Sites

Law careers

Building Career Connections: Networking Tools for Law Students and New Lawyers (Gerson, 2007)

Choosing Small, Choosing Smart: Job Search Strategies for Lawyers in the Small Firm Market (Gerson, 2nd ed., 2005)

Do What You Are: Discover the Perfect Career for You through the Secrets of Personality Type (Tieger, 4th ed., 2007)

Guerilla Tactics for Getting the Legal Job of Your Dreams (Walton, 2008)

Maximize Your Lawyer Potential: Professionalism and Business Etiquette for Law Students and Lawyers (McKim, 2009)

Solo by Choice 2011-2012: How to Be the Lawyer You Always Wanted to Be. (Elefant)

Solo by Choice, The Companion Guide: 34 Questions That Could Transform Your Legal Career (Elefant, 2011)

The Articulate Attorney: Public Speaking for Corporate Lawyers (Johnson, Hunter, 2010)

The New Lawyer Survival Guide, Vol. 1: From Lemons to Lemonade in the New Legal Job Market (Hermann, 2012)

The Opportunity Maker: Strategies for Inspiring Your Legal Career (Kaplan, 2008)

The 6Ps of the BIG 3 for Job-Seeking JDs (Ellis, 2010)

Lawyer well-being

Lawyer, Know Thyself: A Psychological Analysis of Personality Strengths and Weaknesses (Daicoff, 2004)

Mindfulness for Law Students: Using the Power of Mindfulness to Achieve Balance and Success in Law School (Rogers, 2009)

The Contemplative Lawyer: On the Potential Contributions of Mindfulness Meditation to Law Students, Lawyers and Their Clients (Riskin, 2002)

Emotional intelligence

Emotional Intelligence and Emotional Toxicity: Implications for Attorneys and Law Firms (The Colorado Lawyer, April 2004)

Emotional Intelligence in Law Practice (Jan. 31, 2010; a series of monthly presentations headed by Robert Chender, the director of the New York City Bar Association's Contemplative Lawyers Group Lawyers and Emotional Intelligence II). Available at http://contemplativelaw. wordpress.com/2010/01/24/lawyers-and-emotional-intelligence/

Emotional Intelligence: Why It Can Matter More Than IQ (Goleman, 2006)

Exhibit Emotional Intelligence at Law School This Fall (Kaplan, Sept. 10, 2010, available at www.law.com/jsp/article.jsp?id=1202471847823&slreturn=1)

Lawyering with Emotional Intelligence: The Key to Greater Success and Satisfaction (Superior Court of California, County of Santa Barbara, Court Administered Dispute Resolution, January12, 2009. Available at http:// www.sbcadre.org/article/detail.asp?artID=86). Dan Schawbel's

Leadership and The Power of Emotional Intelligence (www.forbes.com, Entrepreneurs, Sept. 15, 2011).

Show Off Your Emotional Intelligence During the Legal Recruiting Process (New York Law Journal; July 20, 2010)

Web sites

Consortium for Research on Emotional Intelligence in Organizations (www. eiconsortium.org/index.htm)

Small Firm Newsletter (www.law.com)

Susan Gainen's blog (www.PasstheBaton.biz)

The Lawyering Survival Guide (www.Lawyerist.com)

Resource Articles for the Career Services Office

1. Small Firm Week...Five Years Later
By Samantha C. Williams, Esq.

The fall of 2007 marked our first Small Firm Week, an important milestone at the Sandra Day O'Connor College of Law at Arizona State University.

The goal in creating a series of educational workshops and networking events relating to small firms was two fold: one, educate students on the small firm hiring process and connect them to potential employers; and two, provide small firms with a presence at the law school and an opportunity to meet students in a low-pressure environment. We gained a tremendous amount of insight from our triumphs (60 students at the career fair!) and our failures (no-shows at speed networking), which I discussed with my fellow NALPers in the article, *Small Firm Outreach: A Two-Way Street* (NALP Bulletin, February 2008).

Fast-forward to 2011, and the completion of five years of Small Firm Week programs and events. We worked hard to expand our numbers over the years, and thus far have brought more than 250 small firm practitioners to campus; presented more than 30 substantive workshops, events and programs; educated more than 800 students on the ins-and-outs of small firm practice; and connected more than 600 students with small firm attorneys around the state.

As you can imagine, these numbers were hard-won, but we learned some important lessons about what works and what doesn't when it comes to connecting students with potential small firm employers. Here's more of the good, the bad, and the ugly:

Timing is everything. Getting your students to attend workshops on any subject matter is always a challenge. You can schedule events months in advance and plan every last detail, but if a popular student organization schedules something against you at the last minute, there's not much you can do about it. At the very least, make sure to calendar events way in advance, and let it be known that events are open to all class levels. That way, student organizations and other coordinators might think twice about scheduling against you. One conflict that can sink an otherwise popular event (and one that many CSOs tend to forget about) is a 1L writing deadline. That happened to us this fall. It turned out that all first year students were in the library cranking out a paper the night of our Practice Area Career Fair. So, try to find out ahead of time when memos/briefs are typically due, and avoid scheduling anything immediately prior to that date.

Creating a culture involves a multi-faceted approach. Getting your students to buy in to small firms as a viable career option is challenging for two reasons: one, smaller firms don't get a lot of press (in paper or online); and two, job opportunities tend to fly under the radar. So, it's up to you to create a culture that fosters a friendly small firm atmosphere. How does one create a culture?

- Be consistent when it comes to offering information about small firms (workshops and educational programs) and opportunities (onsite and offsite networking events).
- Advertising an event here and there is not enough.
- Designate a small firm point person in your office. Let it be known that he or she is the "expert" on all things related to small firms.
- Write and publish information both internally (law school Web site; CSO newsletter) and externally (bar association monthly publication, blog posts).

You might also be surprised to learn that local bar associations are often willing to provide coverage of your events, especially if attorney turnout is high. Not only does this type of coverage put your school and CSO in a very positive light, it can have the effect of increasing both student and attorney attendance at future events.

Let workshops evolve based on student need. None of the dozen or so networking workshops I created were ever the same. One semester I focused on attorney follow-up, the next one was how to network in three easy steps. Do your best to find out what students are perceiving as challenging, and address those issues with a how-to workshop. Students will feel like you are not only listening but responding to their needs.

Use data to strengthen CSO programs. Incorporating up-to-the-minute statistics into your presentation or workshop can be very effective when developing programs. Many law students may not realize that the majority of graduates who find jobs in private practice will land jobs with small firms. In fact, small firm placement is on the rise; a fact that you might use to your advantage when communicating a job search strategy to your students.

Don't forget to toot your own horn. It's important to let everyone know what you're doing, in part to give students a sense of all your hard work. and to what you're trying to accomplish. More important, a little publicity can have the added bonus of motivating students into ramping up their own job search efforts! I provide a recap of Small Firm Week to a group of student leaders every semester (with added hopes they will pass the information along to their constituencies). Showing data on the total number of student and attorneys who participated in Small Firm Week events often elicits a "wow" factor. And don't forget to use social media as a tool to advertise your efforts. Facebook and Twitter are great forums for letting everyone (including faculty and senior administration) know about a successful event.

Creative ways to find attorney-participants. Don't just rely on Martindale-Hubbell to identify local small firm attorneys when seeking to populate an on-campus event. That strategy essentially amounts to cold-calling, which is not terribly effective. To find new attorneys for our annual speed-networking event, I usually scour the state bar magazine looking for the creation of new law firms (which almost always take the form of a partnership or small law firm), and for ads that announce attorney accomplishments. This approach gives me an "in" when I call to extend the invitation.

Little things can go a long way. We implemented a raffle after speed-networking last year which turned out to be a big hit. Prizes included College of Law coffee mugs, leather portfolios, water bottles, and luggage tags. None of these items were significant in terms of their dollar value, but the attorneys loved the concept. (Idea: use business cards as raffle tickets). Speaking of business cards, I always send a handwritten thank you note to each attorney after an event. This, of course, is a time-consuming effort, but it's also a personal touch that can yield positive results.

By Samantha C. Williams, Esq. (NALP Bulletin, April, 2012)

2. Small Firm Outreach: A Two-Way Street
by Samantha C. Williams, Esq.

Career services professionals struggle to bridge the gap between the next small firm associates and the firms that are seeking them.

The Sandra Day O'Connor College of Law Career Services Office at ASU recently coordinated a series of events which culminated in a very successful Small Firm Week. Because small firm outreach continues to be so challenging, insights from our triumphs and failures may be helpful to other career services professionals engaged in similar efforts. Our events were coordinated around an educationally based theme designed to meet many of the challenges career service professionals face when working to create small firm opportunities. We found that coordinating the events all within a one-week period kept the buzz flowing and students interested.

The goal. After the fall recruitment rush, many students and small firms are left asking the question, "What about us?" Students seeking positions with small firms often have no idea how to go about the process.

We offered Small Firm Week to educate students on the small firm employment process. Events during the week showed students how to network effectively in a short amount of time (speed networking); how to build and manage an array of contacts (a speaker specializing in relationship building); how to find a job with a small firm (a panel of small firm attorneys); and what it's like to practice a particular area of law in a small firm (a practice area career fair). After these events, students reported to us that they felt more confident at many different levels.

Small firms often feel disconnected from the law school hiring process because they have no formal recruitment season and hire on an as-needed basis. Educational events such as speed-networking and practice area career fairs give small firms an opportunity to meet students in an unpressured environment. These events also give small firms a chance to recruit top-tier talent because students are more likely to apply to a firm with whom they've had some personal interaction. Lastly, lawyers come away feeling like they now have a presence at the law school.

Accomplishing the goal. The logistics behind inviting 30, 40, or 50 lawyers to one event can be staggering but manageable if you incorporate a few tips:

- Start with a list focusing on alumni and previous job posters. Indicate that you're reaching out to them first because of their importance to the law school.

- Phone calls are best! Use a personalized approach when reaching out to small firms. It's time-consuming but the most effective method. Always ask for a referral (either inside or outside the firm) if someone is unavailable.
- Utilize professors and adjuncts as referral sources, especially for career fairs.
- When looking for a lawyer to fill a particular practice area, call or e-mail the chair of your state bar section's executive council. Our experience was that many lawyers were eager for the opportunity to discuss their specialty, and law students appreciated the wealth of knowledge these lawyers offered.
- Not having the benefit of word-of-mouth is particularly challenging when trying to market the events to the student body. The trick is to blast the message across as many different forums as are available, and even to create some! E-mails are just the beginning. We used flyers, posters, and an electronic message board outside the career services office. One particularly effective marketing tool was publishing an article in the student newspaper on, *"Things You Should Know about Small Firms."* The article highlighted important job placement statistics and useful job search tools. A link to the article was also posted on both the career services and law school Web sites.
- Ask professors to promote events, either in class or in their capacity as advisors. We also reached out to all the student organizations, tailoring an e-mail to each organization, highlighting the fact that a lawyer specializing in their practice area would be participating in the career fair. Finally, personal appearances at your school's SBA forum and student organization meetings go a long way toward showing the students how serious you are about promoting the events.

What we learned. Last-minute cancellations are unavoidable, but there are several things you can do to mitigate the damage. Send a series of reminders to your lawyer participants through different media (e.g., e-mail and hard copy correspondence) at least 10 days before your events. A parking confirmation via e-mail about a week before the event was also an effective reminder for our events. Encourage last-minute participation. Mention in your correspondence that replacements are completely acceptable if a lawyer has to back out, especially for events such as speed-networking, where the only limit on the number of student participants is the number of lawyers who attend.

The bottom line. Small firm outreach is most effective when approached as a two-way street between law student and lawyer. Design and promote your events in such a way that both parties interact in a casual environment, and come away feeling more knowledgeable about the other and better prepared to engage in the small firm employment process.

By Samantha C. Williams, Esq. (NALP Bulletin, February, 2008)

3. Preparing Law Students for Small Firm Practice
by Linda S. Calvert Hanson, Esq.

Author note: *In the current economic downturn, career service professionals are finding it increasingly important to focus a portion of their programming on preparing law students for the small firm market. The article below first appeared in the NALP Bulletin in February, 2003, and was the second in a two-part series. It covers how law students can best prepare for, and effectively market themselves to, small firms. It is information that remains timely today.*

For many schools, the starting point may well be to enlighten law students on why they should even consider small firm employment, and to explain how it differs from practice in a large firm. Next, would follow strategies to target the small firm segment, and a consideration of the small firm culture. This approach will provide a better appreciation for the ways that law students can most effectively market themselves to smaller law firms.

Given the current economic situation, a compelling reason to expand employment horizons beyond larger law firms is because, as noted in the NALP pamphlet, "Guide to Small Firm Employment," small firms typically are not as harshly impacted by economic change. This makes the time ripe to penetrate this overlooked market. Besides, most new law graduates are eager to immediately delve into the practice of law.

Generally, small firm practice offers the young associate more autonomy and responsibility, and accelerated hands-on experience in the courtroom and with case management long before a similarly junior associate in a large firm. Also, the small firm case typically is worked by one or two attorneys as opposed to a "team" of lawyers handling a case in a large firm. Another benefit—cited by a number of small firm practitioners—is that they find greater variability in the types of work they perform throughout a routine day, punctuated by more personal interaction with a larger subset of persons and enhanced client contact. And while a sizeable number of small firms focus on general law, they may be more amenable to expanding into new practice areas when a newer associate can establish competency and an ability to draw in a fresh client base.

Apart from considering the worth of practicing in a small-firm law office, it also is important for the law student to gain an appreciation for the dynamics of small firm practice. First, is the recognition that a "small firm" in Chicago may bear no resemblance to a "small firm" in rural Mayberry, for example. NALP defines a "small firm" as a firm with less than 25 attorneys. In many towns a firm comprising 25 lawyers well could be a "large" firm. Therefore, the law students' efforts to effectively market themselves to a small firm will vary depending upon the geographic locale and just how small is small. Also, more small firm hires results from a reaction to a pressing, immediate need rather from meeting long-term goals. This factor has the added value of generating positions outside of the traditional hiring cycle.

Law students cannot rely solely upon advertised positions when seeking small firm employment. Many solo and small firm practitioners are simply too busy to carve out the time to advertise and search for help. Therefore, a considerable challenge arises when trying to identify small firms to target. This fact persuades the law student to be more creative and resourceful when seeking these positions as most law schools are not fortunate enough to have small firm database or to host a small firm job fair (although some law schools' alumnus directories may provide such valuable information).

A search on Martindale-Hubble may be of limited consequences in that many solo and small firm practitioners are not typically listed in this database. One means to locate small firms is to access the "Solo and Small Firm" sections of the American Bar Association, the state bar, and many local bar organizations. For little to no cost, law schools or law students can obtain the "Solo and Small Firm" sections' mailing lists to prepare a targeted mailing, although again, not all small practitioners join such sections. The prudent law student would obtain a student membership to the section and attend CLE seminars focused toward general and small firm practitioners. But the diligent law student could post a "law student available for legal research & drafting" notice at the local law library. This tactic may prove particularly helpful because small firm attorneys are less likely to have a full in-house library or complete legal database subscription, thus, are more likely to use this resource.

Other ways to locate small firms include the more traditional methods such as networking, and letting it be known that the student is interested in gaining small firm experience. Another option is to join the local bar association where the student can offer to assist with registration or volunteer to write an article or summary of a recent important case. Students should be aware, however, that small firm practitioners may be less able to sacrifice time to attend a bar luncheon, so it may not prove to be fertile ground for meeting the small firm practitioners. More unconventional approaches include observing a hearing, and then engage the attorney with a comment about a particular technique, or to ask a question after identifying themselves as an inquiring law student. They could then volunteer to research the motion the judge just set for hearing conveying a "can do" attitude. It would be tough for most small firm attorneys to turn down free help and the student can always follow up with, "Once you have the product, if you'd like, you can pay me what you think it is worth."

An approach to demonstrate a law student's initiative would be to make a "cold call" to the small law firm, armed with information on the firm and a resume. Students do get hired by small firms this way. They may want to be mindful, however, that to get past the "gatekeeper," they must make a good visual presentation, display a friendly demeanor, and be willing to persistently follow up.

By Linda S. Calvert Hanson, Esq. (NALP Bulletin, February, 2003)

APPENDIX F

Endnotes

Chapter 1

These statistics are collected each year as all of the 200 ABA-accredited law schools report their nine-month post graduation employment statistics to the American Bar Association and to NALP, the Association of Legal Professionals.

Chapter 16

1. NALP Foundation Survey of Law Firm Use of Core Competencies and Benchmarking in Associate Compensation and Advancement Structures 2010.
2. Peter B. Sloan, *From Classes to Competencies, Lockstep to Levels.* 2002: Blackwell Sanders Peper Martin LLP Bock, Heather, and Robert Ruyak, Constructing Core Competencies: Using Competency Models to Manage Firm Talent. 2007: American Bar Association, Chicago, IL.

Chapter 18

American Bar Association Task Force on Law Schools and the Profession: Narrowing the Gap. Legal Education and Professional Development—an Educational Continuum (ABA, 1992 at p. 142).

Chapter 20

Lawyering with *Emotional Intelligence. The Key to Greater Success and Satisfaction* (David C. Peterson, JD, LLM, MDR January12, 2009), Superior Court of California, County of Santa Barbara, Court Administered Dispute Resolution, www.sbcadre.org/article/detail.asp?artID=86.

Made in the USA
Lexington, KY
21 May 2013